RETAIN

How to Create an Incredible
Company Culture that No One
Wants to Leave

By **DREW HARDEN**

ISBN: 9798377050872

Contents

INTRODUCTION

Working at a positive, supportive company is a truly amazing experience.

Unfortunately, that wasn't what I was experiencing.

For years, I had seen my employer's company culture deteriorate. My team members were constantly talking negatively about one another. People were looking over their shoulders to ensure their credit wasn't stolen. No one seemed interested in helping others. Gossip and drama were rampant.

And the leaders of the company didn't seem interested in fostering a better work environment.

I remember driving home from the office back in those days feeling worn out due to the toxic culture. I knew I wanted a better quality of life in my work environment, but I wasn't sure how that could be accomplished. I was young and inexperienced, just a few years out of college, and had no idea how to improve a workplace environment.

So I decided to take a drastic approach. I had been considering moving into the new and growing digital marketing industry for a while. This seemed like the perfect time to start over and build a great company culture from scratch. Everyone wants to work in a positive, supportive work environment. How hard could it be?

4

I left the company and co-founded Blue Compass, one of the Midwest's first digital marketing agencies. One of our founding principles was to simply have a fun, positive work environment.

Thankfully, Blue Compass was a hit. We were blessed with growth, and shortly after our launch in 2007, we grew from two to eight team members. Things were very exciting in those early days as we added clients and made an impact in our market. The best part, however, wasn't the new projects or even the growing revenues. It was the culture.

Coming to work each day was a joy. And it wasn't just me - everyone felt that way. Our work environment was filled with laughter and was incredibly supportive. We all cared about each other and went out of our way to help one another. Our goal to have an amazing company culture had been realized, and it wasn't particularly difficult to accomplish.

Then the best and worst thing that ever happened to Blue Compass occurred.

We won a huge new project. It was the biggest account we had experienced. I was ecstatic. This opportunity would surely push us to new heights!

We immediately doubled in size from eight to sixteen team members. While the growth we were experiencing was truly exciting, I began to notice something troubling.

Our company culture was no longer positive.

Gossip began to creep in. The drama was escalating. We had hired too fast, and many of our new employees weren't the right fit for our team.

I realized the power of my personality wasn't enough to sustain a positive company culture. Now that we had more employees, a deliberate plan was needed.

Great company culture doesn't just happen. It has to be purposefully created and sustained. But how?

I became obsessed with resurrecting the incredible work environment that once was. It set me out on a journey of workplace culture exploration. I began reading books, seeking expert advice, and experimenting with strategies to improve the work lives of our team members. Can positive company culture be produced and maintained? Is there a recipe for a fun work environment? Or are organizations and humans simply too flawed to sustain a long-term, positive company culture?

Today, many years later, with continued company growth and dozens of team members, I'm happy to say the answer is, "yes." We, along with a number of other great organizations, have discovered the secret to a positive, fun supportive company culture that attracts and retains great talent.

Today, we regularly have clients compliment us on how happy and positive our team members are. People who enter our office regularly remark that they can feel the positive energy. We frequently win awards for our incredible culture. We literally receive business from new clients because of our culture. Other organizations ask to meet with us in order to learn how we maintain our culture. I'm regularly interviewed about culture on podcasts and by the media. I'm asked to speak about our culture at conferences and events. And I have the opportunity to consult with other companies to improve their workplaces.

Our employee retention is strong, despite the fact that our team members are regularly sought after by competitors and headhunters. I just learned that four of our team members were recently contacted by a competing agency, asking them to interview. They said, "no." Meanwhile, one of the team members at this agency just reached out to us, seeking to join our team.

After three months of employment at Blue Compass, team members undergo a 90-day review. In this meeting, we ask a number of questions and record the employee's responses. One of the questions is: "Is working at Blue Compass what you expected?" Over 95 percent of the time the answer is the same, "Working at Blue Compass is much better than I could have expected."

For me, that's the most important result of great company culture. I want our team members to feel 100 percent supported. I want them to have the freedom to take creative risks and do great work. I want them to appreciate and value one another. I want them to feel joyful.

We're not perfect. Even Blue Compass has a little drama show up from time to time. But I believe we've cracked the company culture code. Your organization can do the same.

Transforming your company's culture likely won't be easy. It can be challenging, and it can take a while. But it is absolutely possible. We've turned our culture around. We've replaced the drama with encouragement and the gossip with laughter. We've created an environment and a mindset that frees us from the fear of team members leaving.

And you can too.

You don't have to be a CEO to change company culture, but you do have to be a leader. Thankfully, your title doesn't make you a leader; your actions do. And real leaders aren't simply masters of the bottom line and industry experts. They focus their time and energy on crafting an incredible company culture that allows everyone to grow, flourish, enjoy, and accomplish.

This book is the culmination of my journey to improve the culture of companies everywhere. These principles are applicable whether your organization has three employees or 30,000. Whether you have a full office of people, a remote office, or a hybrid of the two. These aren't theoretical concepts that sounded good to me. I'm not a theoretical thinker who thought up a few principles that sound clever. I'm a business owner who leads a team of dozens of full-time people each and every day. I know these ideas work because we successfully use them daily.

First, we'll explore what truly great company culture is and what benefits it will bring your organization. I'll share a number of examples of what we've done to improve our workplace (including a particularly crazy story in chapter 4). Then, I'll reveal the Five Keys of Incredible Company Culture and how they can impact your organization. I'll share how to hire the right people, provide tips specific to remote offices and reveal how your culture can attract prospective clients and employees.

The truth is, you can't have a perfect workplace. That doesn't exist.

But you can experience a better culture that improves morale, loyalty, and the bottom line. You can create a joyful workplace with clear values where team members experience incredible connections, appreciation and growth. You can develop a work environment that rejects drama and gossip.

And you can create an incredible company culture that no one wants to leave.

CHAPTER 1
A PING PONG TABLE DOES NOT EQUAL GREAT COMPANY CULTURE

"Corporate culture is the only sustainable competitive advantage that is completely within the control of the entrepreneur. Develop a strong corporate culture first and foremost." - David Cummings

Leave it to me to strike up a conversation about company culture at a fourth of July parade. I was with my family at an Independence Day celebration in Adel, Iowa. As we watched the floats, high school marching band, and patriotic tractors slowly make their way by, I began talking with the older gentleman standing next to me.

He had just retired after working at a corporation for 42 years. I expressed my congratulations. "42 years is very impressive! That's incredible loyalty." He was appreciative of the comment but didn't remain positive for long. "People don't stick around much at their jobs anymore," he said. "They aren't loyal, and businesses don't do anything to keep them around."

Sadly, he had a good point.

A Satisfaction and Retention Problem

Job hopping has become common. The average amount of time a person in the US stays at a job is about 4.1 years, and only 3.2 years for younger workers ages 25 to 34.[1]

Many people today simply aren't satisfied with their jobs. But why this dissatisfaction? Numerous corporations are wondering the same thing and asking, "How do we stop employees from leaving?"

That's a good question. But it's also the wrong question.

The workforce has changed significantly over the last few decades. As the generations of workers have changed, so have their preferences. What people value in a workplace has changed. We want more from our jobs today than we ever have before.

Years ago, our jobs were just a part of our lives. We spent more time socializing with friends and neighbors outside of work. We gained our sense of purpose from family and church. When we left work, we left work. We weren't constantly connected.

Today, work has become our place to socialize, our source of therapy and our source of purpose. Our jobs are our identities. We're constantly connected to our work. Unfortunately, we've lost many of the positive traditions and institutions that have provided the purpose and balance we so desperately need.

Additionally, we now live in an Instagram/TikTok/LinkedIn world where every company's culture looks better than yours. Why? Because social media rarely reflects reality and only portrays the best.

All this puts a much greater strain on employers today.

The truth is businesses can't be everything to every worker, nor should they have to. But that doesn't change the fact that there's more pressure on employers to provide a greater return for employment than ever before.

Businesses are desperate to keep workers from quitting. Retaining talent has become employers' unattainable Holy Grail. Unfortunately, keeping good people has proven to be especially difficult recently. Sensing this, most corporations have tried to get more competitive in their offerings to employees in the last few years.

During the "Great Resignation" of the early 2020s, millions of workers left their jobs for greener pastures. Businesses began scrambling to do whatever they could to keep talent from leaving. Corporations thought they had the answer and unleashed a secret weapon perfectly designed to attract and retain the best employees: tangible benefits. More PTO, in-office gyms, extra holiday time off, longer maternity/paternity leave and remote work options were rolled out in an attempt to appease workers and convince them to stick around for years to come.

Extra benefits are wonderful. It's good to see organizations offering more options for employees. However, it hasn't helped. In just one year, 47 million people left their jobs,[2] and 40 percent of workers are currently considering leaving their employers.[3] Throwing more PTO at people rarely results in a happy, productive workforce that stays employed for years to come. These offerings are nice, but they're not unique, and they don't make the workday itself more supportive, collaborative, or positive.

In fact, most people value a positive, engaging work environment more than perks, benefits or even salary.[4] In my experience, this seems to be particularly true of younger generations, who seem to value experiences more than things.

Years ago, Timothy Judge, a business professor at the University of Florida, set out to determine the real impact of salary on job satisfaction. He combined 86 different studies and examined the effects of pay on more than 15,000 employees. The result? Level of pay had almost nothing to do with job satisfaction.[5] Offering a strong, competitive salary is extremely important, but it's not the long-term fix for employee retention.

The right question for organizations to be asking isn't, "how do we stop employees from leaving?" We should instead be asking, "how can we allow good people to grow, flourish and enjoy their work?" If we can answer that question, we need not worry about people leaving our organizations.

Thankfully, there's a clear answer to this fantastic question: great company culture.

A positive, supportive, fun work environment is the ultimate competitive edge. I've seen a great culture keep good people happy for decades, directly win more business for companies and allow small businesses to hire impressive talent away from big corporations offering better salaries and benefits. An outstanding company culture can improve every aspect of your working life. As marketer Brian Kristofek says, "Being a great place to work is the difference between being a good company and a great company."

But that leads us to another important question: what exactly is good company culture?

What Good Company Culture Is... and Isn't

Go to nearly any corporation's website and you will find a page all about their "amazing" culture. You'll likely see photos of employees playing ping pong and enjoying a beer on Fridays. Just about every organization claims it has a wonderful culture.

But a ping pong table isn't good company culture.

Imagine spending the time and money to find and acquire the best seeds for your garden. You carefully plant them expecting a great harvest, but then become busy focusing on other things and do little else to maintain the garden and nurture the seeds. Weeds spring up, the sun scorches and the soil dries out. Most of the seeds fail to sprout. Some die out and those that do survive never truly thrive.

Contrast that with the habits of a skilled gardener. She selects the best seeds and plants them in rich soil. She regularly waters the seeds, ensures they get the right amount of sunlight and removes any weeds that spring up. She is constantly monitoring the quality of the soil to ensure the seeds have the right environment. The seeds grow, flourish and produce.

Company culture isn't an event. It's not a single benefit. It's much deeper than that.

Company culture is the sum of the values, leadership and interactions of your workplace, shaping the overall daily experience for the team.

Truly good culture is something that permeates every minute and every second of every workday. This positive work environment can be felt, whether in a physical office or remote and manifests itself in positive occurrences each and every day. As I mentioned, we regularly have visitors to the Blue Compass office remark that they can feel the positivity when they enter. A great culture can be felt. It's almost like energy in the air.

How do you know when a company has a truly incredible culture? Here are 16 signs of a strong company culture:

1. Team members praise each other.
2. Managers regularly ask how their team members are, then actively listen.
3. No one worries about someone taking away their credit.
4. Departments are not in opposition with one another.
5. Laughter is regularly heard in the office, over calls or during meetings.
6. Compliments are common.
7. There are regular opportunities for personal growth and development.
8. Team members spend time with each other outside of work.
9. Nearly everyone attends optional company hangouts, parties and events.
10. Company leadership offers regular encouragement, direction and support.
11. People are happy on Mondays.
12. Gossip is rare.
13. You leave work feeling positive.
14. You're not constantly working evenings, nights or weekends.
15. Your coworkers feel like family.
16. Retention of your team members is strong.

Are these regular occurrences in your work environment? If so, fantastic! You're already moving in the right direction. If not, you're not alone. Most organizations experience a few of these but lack the majority. In fact, most professionals find it a little unbelievable that all of these could actually be regular occurrences in an organization. But they can! The Five Keys of Incredible Company Culture can help slowly insert these occurrences into your company until they are commonplace.

Your job is to monitor the soil, pull the weeds, water the seeds and ensure there's plenty of sunshine. Your job is to encourage a positive work environment, and you don't have to be the CEO to make it happen.

Culture Trends Toward Negative

It's tempting for leaders to focus on meetings, budgets and checklists while trusting the culture of the organization to take care of itself. While that may have been acceptable in workplaces in the past, it's no longer a viable option.

Humans are flawed. No organization, company, business, tribe or family will ever be in perfect harmony. We are fallen, fallible creatures who require the combination of a strong value system, hope and leadership to be our best.

When left unchecked, workplaces descend into gossip and drama. Most of this conflict stems from self-centered pride. Nearly every issue we humans face comes from pride, which can generate unhealthy competition. "Where there is strife, there is pride, but wisdom is found in those who take advice," according to Proverbs 13:10. As C.S. Lewis wrote in *Mere Christianity*, "Pride gets no pleasure out of having something, only out of having more of it than the next person."

Pride and selfish ambition are enemies of a strong team and an enjoyable workplace. They must be dealt with and replaced with more positive qualities.

Why Go Through All the Effort?

Is creating a wonderful culture easy? Absolutely not. It takes hours, days, months and even years of purposeful planning and effort. Additionally, once a positive work environment is attained, your work doesn't end. It must be continually maintained.

Critics may ask, "Why spend all the time and effort on culture? Wouldn't that be better spent on something more tangible like boosting sales, improving operations, building client relations or increasing quality?"

The answer is simple: you spend all that time and effort because the quality of your culture affects everything. Your culture significantly influences your sales, operations, client relationships, and quality of services and products. A great work environment makes everything better by blessing your most important resource: your people. A broken culture can and will sink an organization.

Organizations that don't just select good team members but focus on giving them a positive, nurturing environment have an incredible advantage that greatly improves all these areas of business. They have more enjoyable and exciting workdays. They are eager to support one another and contribute their best efforts. Higher quality work is delivered, and clients experience positivity because happy, fulfilled employees give better service.

In his book, *Managing the Professional Services Firm*, David H Maister emphasizes this point, stating, "Even the most sophisticated client will... come to focus more heavily on the quality of service than on the quality of work. Because of the ambiguity that surrounds technical excellence (and the difficulty the client has in appraising it), the personal relationship between the client and the provider takes on great significance in all of the professions."

Have you ever found yourself struggling with gossip or drama at your organization? These prevalent office poisons do more to hinder health, relationships and productivity than anything else in business today. Imagine how joyful and productive your team could be if they were fully free of the shackles of gossip and drama.

In his book, *An Everyone Culture*, Robert Kegan explains that in most organizations, each employee is doing two jobs. The first is the public job they're actually paid to do. The second is a very private, unpaid job they do in secret: hiding their individual limitations and weaknesses, watching their backs and combating gossip. Imagine how much more productive and happy employees would be if they didn't have to worry about that second job.

A strong company culture is armor that protects your team against the arrows of modern business. It eases misunderstandings and calms irritation. It promotes trust and allows coworkers to assume the best. Brian Chesky, Co-founder and CEO of Airbnb, put it well when he stated, "Why is culture so important to a business? Here is a simple way to frame it. The stronger the culture, the less corporate process a company needs. When the culture is strong, you can trust everyone to do the right thing." Wise leaders know that a unified, strong culture has a greater impact than new operating procedures, financial goals or marketing strategies.

In the 1980s, Porsche AG Worldwide, the world's largest sports car manufacturer, was struggling. CEO Peter Schutz was tasked with making a deep change or facing possible bankruptcy for the company. Thankfully, Schutz was up for the task and was able to turn the company around.

"The biggest challenge was to restore a dying organization, which was losing money, to growth and profitability," said Schutz in a 2012 interview with *Forbes*. "The first steps were not cutting costs, developing new products and/or services, inventing clever new marketing concepts, or clever advertising! Instead, the first steps were rebuilding a culture where all employees were a family, striving for a "shared" success!"

Simply put, if a business wants long-term profitability, needs employees to stay and desires to provide them with a good quality of life, a positive company culture is absolutely essential.

"I used to believe that culture was 'soft,' and had little bearing on our bottom line," said author Vern Dosch. "What I believe today is that our culture has everything to do with our bottom line, now and into the future."

Who Can Change Culture?
Before we dive into ways to diagnose and improve your culture, it's prudent to address a common concern. One of the questions I often receive is, "I'm not the President or CEO. What can I do to improve our company culture?"

It's a good question because it does take a leader to change company culture. But as I mentioned in the introduction, your title doesn't make you a leader, your actions do. Leadership expert

John Maxwell says, "Leadership is not about titles, positions or flowcharts. It's about one life influencing another." Interns can demonstrate better leadership than c-suite executives. If you're not a President or CEO of a company, don't use your lack of an impressive title as an excuse not to help improve your work environment. The best way to get a behavior from others is to exhibit that behavior yourself.

Will the President, CEO, c-suite executive, VP or business owner have the most influence to change the organization's culture? Absolutely. But if that's not you, these principles can still be modeled for your coworkers and your manager. You have more influence over them than you may think.

Don't let your title or lack thereof determine how much influence you have over the culture of your workplace. The fact is you can impact your organization for the better in deep and meaningful ways (see further thoughts on how to influence company culture without an impressive title in chapter 10).

The Five Keys of Incredible Company Culture
Over the next five chapters, I'll present each one of the Five Keys of Incredible Company Culture. Each chapter will provide unique stories and examples, present the big idea, and share ways you can implement the featured key into your culture.

As you journey through each chapter, consider how well your organization is handling each Key, scoring it between one and 10 for each. This simple grading scale will be helpful to revisit in the next few months as you seek to improve your workplace. Consider how your company can continue doing well where it's strong and improve where it's weak. If your organization is like most, it's doing well following some Keys and struggling with others.

The Five Keys of Incredible Company Culture are:
1. Visible Values
2. Appreciative Acknowledgment
3. Jovial Joy
4. Constant Connection
5. Genuine Growth

Each of these individual principles is powerful in the workplace, but when combined, they can ignite an incredible company culture. Additionally, note that these aren't just qualities of a good culture but character traits of a great leader. The culture of a company is a reflection of its leaders.

MAJOR TAKEAWAYS

- Tangible benefits, such as higher salary, longer maternity/paternity leave and more remote work options, are not keys to great company culture.
- A positive, supportive, fun work environment is the ultimate competitive edge.
- Truly good culture is something that permeates every minute and every second of every workday.
- The quality of your culture affects everything, including sales, client relationships, operations, services or products, etc.
- Gossip and drama are poison to company culture.
- Everyone can impact company culture for the better; not just managers, VPs and the c-suite.
- Your title doesn't make you a leader, your actions do.

- The best way to get a behavior from others is to exhibit that behavior yourself,
- The Five Keys of Incredible Company Culture are:
    1. Visible Values
    2. Appreciative Acknowledgment
    3. Jovial Joy
    4. Constant Connection
    5. Genuine Growth

CHAPTER 2
COMPANY CULTURE KEY #1: VISIBLE VALUES

"Culture is a thousand things, a thousand times. It's living the core values when you hire; when you write an email; when you are working on a project; when you are walking in the hall." - Brian Chesky

After standing for an hour in front of video camera lights, my smile was starting to wane. Sweat was forming on my forehead, and my feet were starting to feel sore. Three team members and I were standing on our conference center stage, presenting to a dozen members of the marketing department of a large corporation on a video call. We were one of three finalists attempting to win a big website project. Hopefully our well-rehearsed pitch, along with the professional stage and killer lighting, would give us the edge.

I was optimistic about our chances. We had put together a powerful slide deck showing exactly how we would serve the prospect and why we were the best digital marketing agency to do so. We had built effective websites like this many times before, and I knew we could knock this project out of the park.

The presentation seemed to go well. We each presented our part, then expertly answered their questions. The prospect thanked us for our time and told us we'd hear back from them within a week. Sadly, however, one week turned into two and two into three. I knew the longer we didn't hear from the prospect, the worse our chances became.

Indeed, after three weeks, we received the news that the prospect had selected another vendor. We asked what we could have done better, as we always do when we lose a project. "Nothing," said the VP of Marketing, "you did a fantastic presentation, and we're impressed with your skill set. The only reason we didn't choose you is your size. We feel your firm is too small for a project of this size." With that, the corporation awarded the project to a large agency with hundreds of employees in a larger city.

I felt frustrated. We had handled projects much bigger than this in the past. Not only were we large enough to succeed on this project, we could have succeeded with a project ten times this size. As a business owner who started a company with just two employees, I'm no stranger to having my agency be considered too small. But when this pitch occurred, we had over 30 team members and could easily handle the project. In fact, we had recently lost another project because we were considered too big by another potential client.

While I wallowed in a bit of frustration, something magical happened. "We have such a great presentation now," said one of our Account Executives. "This slide deck is awesome. It will come in handy in our next presentation." Another team member chimed in, "At least they know who we are now. I can see them coming back to us for other projects in the future."

Those comments changed my perception and attitude. I'm known as a positive person around our office, but even I need encouragement to look at the bright side every now and again. We didn't win the project, but what we had learned and created along the way was incredibly valuable.

Why did our team react so positively to this clearly negative outcome? The reason is simple: positivity is in our nature. It's baked into our culture. It's in our DNA. This leads us to generally respond positively when we're faced with a tough situation.

How did we sew such deep seeds of positivity into our culture? We established it as one of our values, and we haven't forgotten it.

The Foundation for a Strong Culture
The first essential key to a truly excellent organizational culture is clear, frequently-articulated company values. There is great strength in deciding what your organization stands for and holding fast to these principles. Well-thought-out values give your team guideposts by which to conduct themselves each day. Establishing clear guidelines helps remove the confusion that may creep into day-to-day activities. Core values are the foundation of a positive culture.

As past CEO of Zappos, Tony Hsieh says, "Your personal core values define who you are, and a company's core values ultimately define the company's character and brand. For individuals, character is destiny. For organizations, culture is destiny." Indeed, your organization's core values will determine its attitude, trajectory and, ultimately, destiny.

New York City restaurateur and the CEO of the Union Square Hospitality Group, Danny Meyer says, "It's the job of any business owner to be clear about the company's nonnegotiable core values. They're the riverbanks that help guide us as we refine and improve on performance and excellence. A lack of riverbanks creates estuaries and cloudy waters that are confusing to navigate. I want a crystal-clear, swiftly flowing stream."

How We Started to Turn Our Culture Around

In the intro of this book, I shared that many years ago, our culture had become negative. Gossip and drama had crept in, and we realized we had to get serious about changing our work environment if we wanted the benefits of a positive culture.

Our first move was to select and define five core values. Today, our values form the foundation of our culture and are the bedrock of the great work environment we enjoy today.

These are our five value statements:

WE ARE POSITIVE. We selected this value because we want to be a team that focuses on the positive instead of dwelling on the negative. Being positive makes our lives more enjoyable. If something goes wrong, we want to learn from it and move on. It's human nature to be stuck in negativity, but there is simply more joy and opportunities in looking at the bright side. Occasionally we'll hear people criticize positive thinking for being unrealistic and overhyped. But as master motivator Zig Ziglar once said, "Positive thinking won't let you do *anything,* but it will let you do *everything* better than negative thinking will."

WE GROW OUR EXPERTISE. We chose this value because we know that both our people and our company must move forward. As former football coach and player Lou Holtz once said, "In this world, you're either growing, or you're dying." Digital marketing trends such as Google's search algorithm and Facebook's user experience are constantly changing. We must commit to increasing our expertise because our clients depend upon it. Learning grows our team, our clients, and our opportunities.

WE SUPPORT ONE ANOTHER. This value is my favorite. If you want to join our team, you must be supportive and encouraging. We don't want superstars. We want team players. Blue Compass isn't a good place to work if you're looking for personal glory. No one should ever have to watch their own back; that's their coworkers' job. One simple way I see this value manifest itself is when a team member is working past 5:00 pm I almost always hear someone else say, "what can I do to help?"

WE GIVE CLIENTS OUR BEST. Of course, it's all about growing our clients' businesses and bringing them success. We selected this value not only to emphasize the importance of delivering high-quality work but the attitude behind our work. We're not here just to do work but to produce meaningful results through our best efforts. We wouldn't exist without our clients. We owe them our absolute highest quality work. I believe all work can be viewed as a higher calling, "Whatever you do, work at it with all your heart, as working for the Lord, not for human masters," according to Colossians 3:23.

WE REJECT DRAMA & GOSSIP. This is most people's favorite value. Everyone loves the idea of work without drama and gossip. While gossip can build a brief, fleeting bond between people because of shared dislikes, it has terrible lasting results. Working in an office or remote environment with gossip and drama is a stressful, taxing experience. Is Blue Compass 100 percent drama and gossip free? No, and I'm not sure it's possible to work at such a place. But we're close. One of our newer team members recently said to me, "I can't believe there's no drama here. I don't understand it." That's music to my ears. We are committed to an enjoyable, drama-free work environment.

These values are hanging prominently on our office wall. They can be found on our website. I regularly post about them on my social media accounts. I frequently reference them when speaking with our team. They help guide our actions and define who we are. I love having them front and center, as it ensures they're always top of mind.

Do you need these five values on your wall? Are these the perfect values for every organization? Of course not. Every company is different, but these have worked well for us.

Believe it or not, absolutely every organization has a set of core values. Some adopt their values, while others let values adopt them. Strong organizations set and stick to specific values. Weak organizations don't take the time and effort to set values, but they still follow a set of convenient, non-verbalized principles. Just because you don't write your values on the wall doesn't mean you don't have values.

If your organization is new or if it's very small, it's likely you've not yet defined your values. If your organization is like most, however, it has a few values, but they're not really talked about, nor are they often followed.

In this next section, I'll briefly show you how to define your organization's core values (even if you have solid values established, stick with me; understanding the value-selection process will give you the ability to better understand and articulate yours). Next, we'll explore ways you can better promote your values to the team in interesting and encouraging ways. Finally, we'll look at ways to use your values to empower your hiring and review process.

The Right Values Lead to the Right Business Decisions

Right after we had adopted our five values, our leadership was put to the test. We had been working for a national technology company that had become our second-largest client, bringing in hundreds of thousands of dollars every year. We interacted with their marketing team daily and were given the task of generating creative social media and content marketing campaigns while guiding their website's search engine optimization.

Working with this profitable client may sound like a great experience, but there was a pretty big catch: the client was incredibly difficult. They were untrusting and questioned everything we did. They were demeaning and unkind to our team members. While the relationship was great for the bottom line, it was clearly having a negative impact on our team. We did what we could to improve the relationship, but it eventually became clear that the client wasn't going to improve.

Throughout these struggles, our new values continued to recur in my mind, with one in particular sticking out: "WE SUPPORT ONE ANOTHER." Was it supportive to allow this client to mistreat our team? The answer was clear, and we knew what we had to do: fire our client. This was a difficult and stressful situation. We had never fired a client before. How would they react? Is it a smart business decision to remove our second biggest source of income? Will we be able to replace this business? Will our company survive?

We called the client, and expressed our appreciation for the partnership but told them this clearly wasn't working. We valued our team's mental health and needed to part ways. The client was shocked. I remember our main contact pleading with us to reconsider. That was a very tempting thought, but deep down, I knew this situation wouldn't get better. This client wasn't compatible with our values and the culture we desired to maintain. We fired our first client.

I remember walking out of that conference room and announcing to our team that we would no longer be working with that client. It was as if a weight was immediately lifted. Smiles and rejoicing spread across the office. It was a powerful moment in which I truly realized people are more important than profits, and our team realized we had their back.

What looked like a bad decision on paper was one of the best business decisions I ever made. It strengthened our culture with positive, long-lasting effects. And as a bonus, one hour after this event, we received a call from a current client wanting a proposal for a huge new project. Then later that afternoon, another client called wanting to start a large new marketing campaign.

I believe everything happens for a reason, and we ended up being blessed for making the right decision. We were able to make that decision because we had selected and focused on our company values.

Perhaps you're considering establishing your organization's core values for the first time, reworking your current values, coming up with values for just your department or even selecting your own personal set of core values. Regardless, the first step is to ask, "what do I want to be surrounded by each day?"

The Value Brainstorm Exercise

"The Value Brainstorm" is a powerful exercise consisting of three simple steps that will unveil the values that matter most to your organization. As John Maxwell says, "your core values are the deeply held beliefs that authentically describe your soul." This exercise will help reveal those beliefs.

Step 1 - Bring together a few trusted team members. Depending on your company, as few as two or as many as a dozen may be appropriate. Prepare a whiteboard or Google Doc and assign one person to be the notetaker. Schedule an hour for the activity (depending on your situation and the people involved, may take as little as 30 minutes, but plan for 60 to be safe).

Step 2 - Ask the question, "What are your favorite successes we've experienced as a team?" Write down the answers in brief statements or sentences. For instance, your answers could look like the following:

- The honest conversation with the prospect that won us the big account last summer
- Celebrating our 10th anniversary with a party bus
- Laughing at Todd when he sang at the company party
- Traveling to Singapore with our favorite client and sharing insights at their annual conference
- Receiving such heartfelt gratitude from John's family when they received our gift after his diagnosis

- The learning and personal development we acquired from the Q2 team retreat
- The passion the marketing team put into creating the award-winning social media campaign

Generate at least thirty statements and don't worry about being perfect; there are no wrong answers here.

Step 3 - Ask the team to review your list of success statements and shout out the most powerful words that catch their eye. These will typically be feelings, qualities or attributes, and you'll likely have one or two per statement. Write these words as they're called out. Try to generate at least thirty words, and again, don't worry about being perfect; there are no wrong answers here.

Assuming we performed Step 3 with the previous statements, we would generate the following words:
- Honesty
- Celebration
- Laughter
- Insights
- Gratitude
- Personal development
- Passion

Step 4 - Now that you have your prospective values, narrow down the list. Begin by asking the group which 10 words seem least meaningful to your organization. Once you've eliminated these 10 words, cut 10 more. Your goal is to narrow the list to only the most important words.

Even if they've never written down an official set of core values, most companies intuitively know a positive quality or two that pervades their culture. These qualities may make great contenders for your official values. It's likely, however, that your team desires to have values that aren't currently present in your organization. The values you ultimately select don't have to be qualities your organization currently has. They can be aspirational values you strive towards.

Of course, this exercise doesn't have to be completed in one sitting. It may be beneficial to come back the next day and reevaluate your final results with fresh eyes.

How many core values should you ultimately choose? I've seen organizations with as few as three and as many as a dozen. In my opinion, three to five are ideal. While it may feel easier and more inclusive to adopt more values, don't overdo it. If you stand for too many ideals, you don't stand for anything. There's beauty in simplicity, plus having too many values makes memorization difficult. That's a problem because you want your team to know each of these by heart.

Once you've finalized your core values, consider how best to display and articulate them. Perhaps simply listing words like "Positivity, Expertise, Support, etc." is best for your organization. We decided to make our values a bit more personal and action-oriented by choosing the statements, "We are positive, We grow our expertise, We support one another, etc." Whichever way you choose to display your values, be consistent and stick with that theme.

How to Make Your Values More Relevant and Impactful

Creating your values is just step one. Step two, which is just as important, is to implement your values.

The healthiest organizations live their values. Each employee can recite them and doesn't mind doing so. Every person on the team appreciates the values. They are referenced regularly, and they are strived for. Of course, that sounds pretty amazing, but is it actually possible?

If your values really matter, you need to talk about them, display them and provide rewards when they are followed. The worst values are values that aren't followed. Values that aren't followed are no values at all.

Here are six things your organization can do to ensure your values make a difference:

1. **Make your values visible.** Putting your organization's values on the wall, the website or your intranet may sound a little cheesy, but it's the first step to making them matter. Your values must be visible.

    In the digital marketing industry, we regularly reference the importance of allowing website visitors to be able to find what they're looking for on your website in just a click or two. The same principle must be followed when it comes to what your organization stands for. They must be evident and easily accessible.

    Ensure your team can find your values quickly and easily at any time. But they shouldn't just be evident when you're looking for them. Your values should be in places that cause your team to see them at times when they are not looking for them. Out of sight, out of mind.

At Blue Compass, we have our values listed very clearly on five large canvases in the largest, most trafficked area of our office. You can't miss them.

It's clearly essential for employees to see your values, but it's also important for your clients, prospects and the public to know what you stand for. We have them listed on our website, along with brief explanations of their importance. We also feature our values in every proposal we send out to prospects. Our values give a clear picture of what we believe, and we seek clients who appreciate the same ideals.

2. **Reference your values.** The leadership of your organization should regularly reference the company values.

We hold monthly all-team meetings that I typically lead. I always use this time as an opportunity to reinforce our mission and our values.

I used to recite our value statements to the team in these meetings, but over the years, I realized the power of stories and examples. Today, I recite each value followed by an example of a team member who recently did an excellent job of exemplifying that value. For instance, at our last team meeting, I said, "Our first value statement is, "We are positive." We saw Jordan face a challenge when one of our clients brought up a serious complaint that wasn't our fault. Jordan handled this extremely positively by not getting upset, immediately setting up a meeting internally to discuss options, then scheduling a lunch meeting with the client to discuss the matter."

Not only does this practice cause us to be on the lookout for instances of our values being followed, but it regularly reinforces the importance of each value by rewarding worthy team members with a shout-out.

Find a way to regularly reference your company values with your department or team. Make the values part of a weekly or monthly meeting, your company intranet, your newsletter, etc. Anything you can do to positively, regularly reference your values will make them matter more.

3. **Offer rewards when behavior meets values.** One of the best ways to get an attitude or behavior from others is to offer rewards when it occurs. Employee recognition expert Dr. Bob Nelson rightly says, "You get what you reward. Be clear about what you want to get and systematically reward it."

It's easy to focus on what people are doing wrong, but the opposite is actually much more effective. In his book *Whale Done*, leadership expert Ken Blanchard describes the importance of finding people doing things right, not doing things wrong. The more attention you pay to a behavior, the more you get that behavior. "Attention is like sunshine to humans. What we give our attention to grows. What we ignore, withers," states Blanchard.

With gas prices being so high these days, we recently decided to give each of our team members a surprise gift card to a local gas station chain. Instead of simply handing out these gift cards, we included a brief, individualized note referencing a way we had seen positivity from that person lately. This is just a small way to subtly associate our value of positivity with a reward.

Consider how you can reward others for living out your values. It can be a gift card, a coffee, a public shout-out, or even a simple compliment.

4. **Make your values the standard for employee reviews.** Most companies have annual employee reviews in which feedback and assessment are given. While it is important to review employees' results and the value they add to the company, judging performance based on values is also important.

    At Blue Compass, our reviews are quite simple. We provide each team member (including myself) a document with each of our five value statements, as well as a few other questions. Each team member then shares how they lived each value over the previous year, and how they can improve next year.

    For instance, for our "we support our team" value, an employee may state that she did a fantastic job of helping answer the questions of newer team members in her department. Next year, she plans to do a better job of following through on important tasks for the department manager.

5. **Hire by your values.** You've heard that one bad apple spoils the bunch, and it's absolutely true. If you want to enjoy an amazing company culture, you must add positive, supportive people to your team who embrace your values.

When we're interviewing new potential team members, I often tell our team, "You can teach skills, but you can't teach personality." You must add people who believe in your values from day one. Someone may have an incredible resume and great experience, but if you're getting red flags in the interview because the interviewee is arrogant, you mustn't hire. That person isn't going to change. I'd much prefer to hire someone whose skills need a bit of growth over a rockstar who's going to add drama.

If you participate in interviewing new potential team members, ensure your company values are clearly stated. Ask questions based on these values. When interviewing, I list our five values and then ask which the interviewee feels is most important. I ask for examples of how he or she has displayed a certain value in the past. I listen to how interviewees do or don't embrace our values.

Your values are your first defense against the encroachment of a negative workplace. Use them as guideposts to evaluate who is the right and wrong fit for your team.

Check out chapter seven for more insights on hiring for a great company culture.

6. **Live the values yourself.** As the CEO of a company, there are innumerable hats I wear. My role calls for me to be a leader, a mentor, a business strategist, a digital marketer, a project manager, a web designer, and more. Yet I've come to realize that my number one responsibility is actually quite simple: to know our values, to make them

known, to live out our values myself, and to enable others to do the same.

Whether you're a leader in title or in practice, the most important thing you can do to foster a great company culture is to model good, positive company values. Remember, the best way to get a behavior from others is to exhibit that behavior yourself.

MAJOR TAKEAWAYS

- Core values are the foundation of a positive culture.
- Your company values should reflect what your organization wants to be surrounded by each day.
- Your values must be clear, visible, and frequently referenced.
- Employees should be rewarded in some fashion when they live out your company values.
- Your company values should be part of your employee reviews.
- Your hiring process should evaluate candidates based upon how well they embody your values.
- Leaders must know the company values, make them known, and live them out each day.

CHAPTER 3

COMPANY CULTURE KEY #2: APPRECIATIVE ACKNOWLEDGMENT

"No one ever leaves the company because they've been recognized too much." - Patrick Lencioni

Who wouldn't want a nice pair of cashmere shorts for his work anniversary? Jeff was the first team member to reach 10 years with our company (other than my business partner and me), so we knew we had to do something special. He was instrumental in starting our web development department, and we certainly wouldn't be where we are today without him. We wanted to ensure Jeff knew we appreciated him.

I googled ideas for an employee's 10-year work anniversary. A few of the results I received included:
- Make a slideshow
- Send them lunch
- Decorate their workspace
- Gift them time off
- Schedule an on-the-clock party hour

- Give them a personalized mug

What a boring list.

As you might expect, these ordinary, traditional gifts won't do for Blue Compass. We wanted to surprise him and the team with a recognition that was truly unique.

After a little brainstorming, we decided to let our entire team help make the decision. Without Jeff's knowledge, we gave each of our team members a one-hundred-dollar bill and invited them to help us honor Jeff. Employees could do whatever they wanted with the cash as long as it was honoring Jeff. They could simply give him the money, buy a gift with it or compile the funds together to get something big, which is exactly what our team decided to do. The team purchased tickets for a tropical vacation for Jeff and his wife, along with a fancy cashmere beach outfit.

On the day of Jeff's anniversary, we arrived early and set up a full red carpet lined with dozens of balloons and a sign clearly stating this was Jeff's walkway and Jeff's alone. After he arrived, we surprised him with the vacation and a word of thanks from each team member. Grinning from ear to ear, Jeff gave us a heartfelt thank you for the appreciation.

The Power of Appreciation

There's something deeply powerful about being appreciated. We want to matter. We all desire to be valued, to be liked. Genuine, appreciative acknowledgment fulfills this desire.

Proverbs 16:24 states, "Kind words are like honey—sweet to the soul and healthy for the body." Have you ever experienced a rough day, then received a kind word that changed your day? A simple compliment can change the entire course of someone's day or even life. Imagine what could happen if your workplace was overflowing with kind words of gratitude.

Emotions are contagious. When you take the time to recognize a coworker's contributions and show him appreciation, you're blessing him with the encouragement he needs to continue forward. Your positive action is a domino that causes him to feel positive, which will likely be passed on to someone else. One kind act to one individual can have a ripple effect that influences millions of people. Even the simple act of saying "thank you" can have profound effects on others.

Without care and appreciation, humans will deteriorate emotionally. In fact, 79 percent of employees who quit their jobs say that a lack of appreciation was a major reason for leaving.[6]

At Blue Compass, we teach a simple rule: if you have a positive, encouraging thought about someone, don't keep it to yourself. Share it with others. If you think it, say it.

When I hear one of our team members speaking positively about another, I'll often spread what I call "positive gossip" by sharing the positive comments. "Ben was telling me how happy he is to be working with you on this project," I may say. "He appreciates how clear your direction has been. It's made it really easy for him to move quickly." Wouldn't you love to hear a little "positive gossip" about yourself?

Zig Ziglar said it best: "You never know when a moment and a few sincere words can have an impact on a life."

The value of acknowledgment is especially important if your team works remotely. While Blue Compass has an in-person work environment, our team members do work remotely occasionally and certainly did so during the COVID pandemic. We quickly realized how essential communication and appreciation would be during this period as we transitioned to interacting primarily over chat and video calls in 2020.

Laura, our Office Manager began a simple yet very effective practice: each morning, she posted a statement in our team's chat, "Tell us why _____ is awesome," and added the name of one of our team members. It was amazing how quickly people replied to this statement. Almost instantly, positive comments would flood in about that team member's work ethic, personality, sense of humor, expertise, etc. Laura didn't stop there, however. After everyone on our team had been featured, she compiled all the positive comments in cards and sent them to each team member. Receiving these kind, personalized words was a huge blessing for each individual during this uncertain time. It's wonderful to hear positive comments from a manager or a boss, but sometimes it's even more impactful to receive these comments from coworkers.

Only one in three workers in the U.S. feel that they received recognition for doing good work in the past seven days.[7] It's not uncommon for people to feel their contributions are routinely ignored.

Why is acknowledging your team members' contributions so essential? Because everyone needs to know they matter. Everyone needs to know their contributions make a difference. A paycheck is not enough. It must be accompanied by feedback, direction and, perhaps most importantly, gratitude.

The good news is that appreciating others is neither costly nor time-intensive. Yet while it's clear that employee recognition has an incredibly high return on investment, it doesn't seem to occur often in many organizations.

As Anne M. Mulcahy, former CEO of Xerox, stated, "satisfied employees mean satisfied customers, which leads to profitability."

Foster the Mindset of Acknowledgment

National Employee Appreciation Day falls on the first Friday in March each year, and we always make sure to plan something special to honor our team. This year, we booked a huge party bus and surprised our team by taking them all out to lunch, followed by a tour of the city and games in our parking lot.

We also took the time to write and present a unique, humorous poem for each team member. Each poem thanked an employee for his or her service with a little humor thrown in for good measure. For instance, Jay is a wonderful team member who has mentioned to us that he tries to fly under the radar. This doesn't seem to work, however, because he seems to end up in the middle of office laughter for many reasons, including the bold socks he wears each day. Thus, Jay's poem read:

Jay is an incredible team member
In his skills, there's no dispute
But office productivity has declined since he started
Because his socks are so incredibly cute

Jay, we love your skills and expertise
You're talented; you're a star
We only know one thing you've failed at:

Flying under the Blue Compass radar

The day was a hit. Everyone enjoyed the bus, lunch, games, and poems. This experience got us all out of our daily routines and created memories.

(Does sending cards and writing poems sound a little cheesy to you? You're not alone. These gestures aren't for everyone. But they are incredibly impactful for many people. If you're skeptical, check out chapter 10 where I fully address this critique).

My wife, Melíssa, once had a different experience on Employee Appreciation Day. Her manager had no idea it was a special day until someone mentioned it to him on the day itself. Surprised, he said, "Well, let's give people a half day off today." So, an email went out, telling people they could leave early.

Which experience do you think was more impactful? Which showed greater, individualized appreciation?

While it's great that this department allowed its employees to end work early, it was clearly an afterthought. If PTO was the best expression of this organization's appreciation toward employees, it probably would have been better to let people know ahead of time so they could plan their schedules accordingly. Perhaps a few employees had client meetings that afternoon that they couldn't reschedule. People especially appreciate acknowledgment when it's genuine, purposeful and heartfelt. In this case, it wasn't.

Am I saying that Employee Appreciation Day is the key to acknowledgment and you need to plan a huge event with a mega-budget in early March? Absolutely not. The point is, one organization had employee appreciation top-of-mind while the other didn't. The difference is that acknowledgment is simply part of our culture. It's not a question of if we do something on Employee Appreciation Day; it's what we do.

We all get busy. We get caught up in meetings, schedules, to-do lists and emails. It's hard to make time to acknowledge others; unless it's not something you have to make time for. When you're deeply thankful for your team, you'll naturally express it in words and deeds.

The first step to capitalizing on appreciative acknowledgment is to foster an attitude of appreciation. Your organization's leadership should hold a constant attitude of gratitude towards employees, and your team members should feel that same gratitude towards each other.

Have a "we" culture, not an "I" culture. Laura, our VP of Operations, is incredibly passionate about this concept. In our office, you'll frequently hear "we" and "our" but rarely hear "I" and "me." This isn't a rule we've set, it's a natural outgrowth of an appreciative workplace. When your office is team-centric, everyone feels more supported.

Who Needs Acknowledgement?

A few years ago, I accompanied my wife on one of her business trips to Los Angeles. During the trip, her department threw a going away party for her manager, a Senior VP who had been with the company for four years. The company rented a large venue by the beach in Santa Monica with an exquisite meal, full bar, and live music. I was amazed at the time, effort, and budget that went into the event.

Not long after the trip, I was at the company's corporate office, having lunch in their cafe. In the corner, I noticed a dozen employees singing "happy retirement" around an older gentleman and a small cake. The man had worked at the company for 34 years and was retiring at the end of the week.

I was struck by the way the two men were honored. The difference in the budget for these two retirement parties was likely 20 thousand dollars. While there's certainly nothing wrong with throwing an expensive party to honor your Senior VP, the man with a less impressive title who worked at the company for 30 years longer received much less acknowledgment from the company.

Everyone needs to feel appreciated. It doesn't matter if they're an intern or CEO, we all want to matter. People need acknowledgment regardless of their title or how they're compensated.

When it comes to acknowledging others in our organizations, we often forget the people at the "bottom." It's easy to overlook interns, for instance. We feel they don't deserve special recognition because they simply haven't earned it yet. They're just starting out; they need to pay their dues before they are rewarded, right?

There is a lot of truth to those sentiments. In most cases, young people who are just starting out in their careers don't deserve big paychecks and bonuses. Loyalty, hard work and contributions are necessary first. Some younger people brought up in today's modern "everyone's a winner" culture do feel entitled to more than they deserve. But that doesn't mean they don't need positive feedback and appreciation. I can still remember many of the compliments I received when I was an intern. That acknowledgment was of great encouragement to me.

At the other extreme, it's easy to forget to acknowledge managers, VPs, and members of the c-suite. These people already have power and influence. They're receiving big paychecks. They're doing fine! They shouldn't need any thanks from me, right?

It's easy to think that leaders are confident and in control. The truth is, however, that leaders have the same insecurities that all of us face. As the CEO of a company myself, I occasionally struggle with issues that few others see. When I receive the occasional compliment, encouragement or even just a "thank you," it means the world to me.

Not all Appreciation is Created Equal

It's always positive to show appreciation to a coworker, but you can be even more effective if you know what type of appreciation resonates best with each team member.

In his book, *The 5 Languages of Appreciation in the Workplace*, author Gary Chapman explains that not everyone values the same type of acknowledgment. Each person in your organization is different, and some forms of appreciation may be much more valued by an individual than others. If you express appreciation in ways that aren't meaningful to your team members, they may not feel valued. This is because you and your coworkers are likely speaking different languages.

For instance, some people are motivated by words of encouragement. Giving this type of person an extra day of PTO may make his manager feel like he's done a great act of kindness, but it won't make him feel particularly appreciated. Taking this person aside and genuinely praising him for the amazing job that has been done will give him a deep feeling of appreciation.

Some people are more motivated by other languages of kindness, such as acts of service or tangible gifts. Not all types of acknowledgment are created equal. Understanding how each individual in your organization feels most appreciated is important for those who truly desire an incredible office culture.

Ideally, managers have great relationships with all of those in their care and innately know what makes each person feel special. If not, it may be helpful to take a more concrete approach. At Blue Compass, we have each new employee complete an "appreciation questionnaire," which helps us understand that person's preferences. A few examples of questions include:

- What's your favorite type of coffee?
- Where is your favorite place to hang out?
- What makes you feel valued?
- What's your favorite place to shop?
- What's one drink that's always in your fridge?
- What's your favorite type of encouragement?
- What's your favorite ice cream flavor?
- Would you rather receive a written thank you note, public praise, or a gift card?
- What's your favorite sports team?

Answers to these questions help us immediately understand what each employee enjoys and how we can best speak their "gratitude language." We have these in an internal location that anyone can access at any time. Katrina and Mallory worked late a couple of evenings in a row recently, so I looked up their favorite candy, then wrote thank you notes accompanied with Swedish Fish for

Katrina and a Snickers bar for Mallory. It was a small gesture, but individualization made it more powerful.

Communicating appreciation globally across an organization isn't very effective. The best way to acknowledge someone is individually, creatively, and personally.

Creative Appreciation is More Powerful

At Blue Compass, we're best known for our strategic digital marketing and web development, but we also dabble in death-defying stunts.

That's how I found myself staring down at our parking lot from two stories up, legs aching as I crouched on our very open, exposed roof. It had been an hour and 45 minutes of waiting for our Digital Marketing Director, Katrina, to arrive on a chilly October morning just after a thunderstorm.

While the situation wasn't ideal, Cary, my business partner, and I had a good reason to perch atop the roof. A few weeks earlier, we decided to find a unique way to show appreciation to our employees. We designed and printed giant 10-foot by 20-foot banners, each with a team member's photo and a message ("We love working with Mallory" and "David makes us smile," for instance).

We decided to climb to the top of various buildings around the city, create a reason for each team member to arrive at the building, then drop the banner over the side of the building for a fun (but admittedly strange) moment of surprise and gratitude. And, of course, we hid cameras around the area to capture each gratitude banner unveiling on video. The plan was foolproof. What could go wrong?

More time ticked by. I lost feeling in my limbs. The roof was wet and slippery, and the banner was surprisingly heavy. When I initially envisioned this, I assumed there would be a small wall on the roof that we could stand behind. Unfortunately, however, the roof dropped off directly and offered nothing to stop us from sliding over the edge. I prayed that we wouldn't be pulled over the side, falling two stories in our attempt at a little appreciation.

I felt thankful as we finally recognized Katrina's SUV pulling into the parking lot. She was about to be the first employee to receive the surprise gratitude banner experience.

"Let's do this! Now!" I loudly whispered to Cary. Each holding one end of the heavy banner, we heaved the giant print over the side of the building. Thankfully, the banner held together and didn't pull us over the edge. It unrolled to reveal our gratitude message, and Katrina stopped suddenly, looking a bit puzzled as she stared at our stunt. After a few seconds, she finally realized what was happening and laughed and waved (her dog, Mac & Cheese, on the other hand, was not impressed and began barking wildly). Our first gratitude banner was a success.

We proceeded to unveil more banners wherever we could for other team members. Jordan's banner found us on top of a client's office roof during a thunderstorm. Mallory's banner resulted in us climbing a long, swaying ladder on a windy day to reach a particularly high roof. We waited an hour and a half through lunch to unveil Jeff's banner, only to realize he wasn't even in the office that day (we got him the next morning). While each person reacted differently, they all appreciated the random gesture of thanks.

And we lived to tell the tale.

While all positive acknowledgment is an essential key to having a great culture, there's a certain type that's particularly effective: creative appreciation. When your gesture of appreciation is unique, and out of the ordinary, it can have a deeper, longer-lasting impact.

We hold many celebratory events each year at Blue Compass, but everyone's favorite is our annual Christmas party. This event has become legendary for many reasons, one of which is the annual video my business partner and I put together. We always create a fun video as a little surprise for the team (and their plus ones). A few years ago, we wanted to do something to directly recognize each of our team members. Since we absolutely love all the wonderful, diverse personalities of our team members, we decided to write a script and feature each of them in a video, except Cary and I dressed up as and played each person.

We put together a full story about the arrival of our newest team member at the Blue Compass office and how each team member prepared for the big arrival. We purchased wigs, clothes, glasses, accessories and even fake tattoos. We came into the office on a Saturday and filmed for hours. Each of us played about a dozen different team members (we had about 24 team members at the time). The result was a weird, crazy and absolutely hilarious 10-minute narrative that lovingly played upon all our team members' eccentricities. We delighted our team with the video at our party to thunderous laughter and applause (from our team, at least; I think the plus ones thought we were crazy). Our team absolutely loved the result, and to this day, we still rewatch it together at least a few times a year.

Please don't misunderstand; simple words of encouragement and gratitude should certainly be part of your company culture repertoire. But adding a dose of creativity can greatly enhance the effects of standard appreciation. When you add a creative, meaningful flare to employee acknowledgment, it demonstrates a purposeful intent that brings extra meaning to the gesture. While sayings like "thanks" or "you're doing a great job" are indeed critical, they don't require the thought or planning of an innovative display of appreciation. That's what makes creative appreciation so powerful.

My wife once reached an anniversary with her employer and was sent a $100 DoorDash gift card, as all employees receive on their anniversaries. That's absolutely a great sign of appreciation, but would it be more effective if it was more creative and personalized? We do something similar at our organization, except we give our managers the task of using that money to purchase a personalized gift for the employee. One of our front-end developers recently received a gift card to a woodworking shop, as he's very passionate about woodworking. Another developer received a T-shirt and PlayStation gift card, while one of our project managers was given a gift card to a local cheese bar.

One-size-fits-all isn't ideal when it comes to acknowledging the individuals on your team. Consider ways you can add personalization and creativity to employee acknowledgment.

MAJOR TAKEAWAYS

- No one ever left a company because they were valued too much.
- We want to matter, to be valued and to be liked. Genuine, appreciative acknowledgment fulfills this desire.

- Your organization's leadership should hold a constant attitude of gratitude towards employees.
- Individualized acts of appreciation are much more effective than communicating appreciation globally across an organization.
- The best way to acknowledge someone is individually, creatively and personally.
- Adding a creative flare to employee acknowledgment demonstrates a purposeful intent that brings extra meaning to the gesture.

CHAPTER 4
COMPANY CULTURE KEY #3: JOVIAL JOY

"People rarely succeed unless they have fun in what they're doing." - Dale Carnegie

After spending hours in the car, I turned off the interstate and onto a small country road surrounded by fields of corn and soybeans. I was on an important work trip, but not for a client meeting, industry conference, or business deal. The destination was the living room of one of our team member's parents.

When I arrived, I was greeted with a hug from our employee's mom and a handshake from her dad. We moved into the living room and sat down. I soon found myself listening to stories of her childhood.

While this certainly wasn't a typical professional work meeting, it was an incredibly meaningful experience.

At Blue Compass, we love our team members. Our team is like a family, and we enjoy sharing stories together and learning more about each other. One of the goals of our leadership team is to always look for ways to encourage, surprise and delight our team members.

One afternoon, my business partner, Cary and I were discussing ways we could add a little joy to our office. It had been a particularly busy few months, and it seemed like a morale boost was in order. As we talked, it occurred to us that one of our team member's parents were in from out of state. Wouldn't it be interesting (and funny) if we interviewed them about their daughter? It sounded like a great idea, but then we took it a step farther. "Why only interview one employee's parents? Why not every employee's parents?"

So we decided to secretly meet our team members' parents.

Only our Office Manager, Laura, was aware of our plan. She contacted our team members' parents (unfortunately, to make this endeavor possible, we had to scale down to about 10 sets of parents). She ensured this was comfortable for them and told them to keep our visit a secret. She scheduled the dates for us to arrive at their houses and put together a spreadsheet with directions, addresses, and exact times at which to arrive and leave each home.

Cary and I booked our calendars with events we hoped wouldn't sound too suspicious and drove to the parents' homes over the course of three days (and shout-out to my wife, Melíssa, who accompanied us and filmed everything). We visited parents in cities, suburbs, small towns and farms. Each time we arrived at a home, we were welcomed with open arms, smiles, and hugs.

We asked the parents what each employee was like in high school, what they thought their son or daughter would be when they grew up, and the qualities they loved most about their son or daughter. Our goal was to brag a bit about each person to their parents, then simply learn more about each team member (it was very surprising how forthcoming the parents were with embarrassing stories). Shortly after the trip, we edited the footage and excitedly looked for the perfect moment to share it with the team.

These three days were one of the most wonderful experiences of my professional career. To meet the parents and learn so much more about these team members, who I value so much, was extremely rewarding. My appreciation and gratitude for each of them grew.

A few weeks later, at a gathering of our entire team, I said, "It's incredibly important for all of us to appreciate and understand one another, and what better way for us to understand you than to meet your parents? So, that's what we did." I stepped aside and began to roll the video.

It's certainly not unusual for us to do something unique and out-of-the-ordinary at Blue Compass, but it was evident the team wasn't quite buying the idea that we actually went to visit their parents. As the video started, however, it became clear this was a reality.

Everyone gasped as we pulled up to the first parents' house and entered. As the video continued, the look on each person's face was absolutely priceless. It was a combination of fascination, joy, confusion and anticipation. With the reveal of each new home visit, everyone wondered if his or her parents were next. The team was absolutely ecstatic. We all laughed together as we discovered new stories about each other. Every team member whose parents we visited loved the experience. It was incredibly heart-warming (and yes, we did keep a slightly embarrassing story or two in the video, but they were well-received).

Was this a weird thing to do? Absolutely. Why did we take so much time away from our meetings and to-do lists to drive over 500 miles to secretly meet these parents?

Because we wanted to bring joy to our team!

The experience surprised and delighted our team. It helped us better understand and appreciate each other. And it showed our company's leadership cared enough to take the time and effort to actually spend time with employees' families. It has provided us with countless memories that we still laugh about today.

While we originally never considered making this experience public, we eventually placed a short, employee-approved video of the experience online (if you'd like to check it out, visit **drewharden.com/culturevideos**).

Joy Unlocks Healthy, Successful Work Culture

When you take the time and effort to bring joy into your office, great things happen. Do you have to perform a large-scale, crazy "meet the parents" style scenario like this to have a great workplace? Of course not. Little moments of joy can be just as powerful. In fact, regular small doses of fun lead to a strong company culture.

In the movie *Top Gun: Maverick*, the lead character Maverick (played by Tom Cruise) is training a team of skilled pilots for an incredibly important mission that could save the lives of millions of people. Unfortunately, he has very limited time to teach the pilots what they need to know. Strangely, with only a week until the mission, he stops the training and lets his team unwind with a lively game of football on the beach.

As the game proceeds, Maverick's superior officer approaches and asks why he's wasting time when there's such an important deadline just days away.

"You said to create a team, sir," replies Maverick. "Here's your team."

You can't have a truly successful team without strong relationships. You can't have strong relationships without bonding. And one of the best ways to bond is to have fun together.

Maverick knew that playing together would cause his team to bond. He knew that taking their minds off work for a while would cause them to feel rejuvenated. Sometimes not working is the most productive thing your team can do together.

Who's the most popular employee at your organization? At ours, the answer is simple: Mac & Cheese. Who is this beloved team member? Mac is our "Digital Barketing Manager," a clever (or cheesy?) play on the title "Digital Marketing Manager." He's a golden retriever who spends each and every day in our office.

But Mac has competition.

Wrigley, Desi, Mozzarella, and Nala are a few of the other dogs vying for the attention of our team and our clients.

Our dog friendly office is loved by employees and clients alike. It's one of the most popular aspects of our culture. Do the dogs occasionally get a little loud and boisterous? Absolutely. But it's a simple way that we've chosen to add a little joy to our culture.

"Surround yourself with people who take their work seriously, but not themselves, those who work hard and play hard," Colin Powell once said.

It's been estimated that you will spend roughly one-third of your life at work. Life is too short not to enjoy the workplace. It's paramount for employers not only to accept a fun work environment but to create a fun work environment. Choose to be purposeful about adding joy to your organization.

How healthy is your office culture? It's hard to judge, but here's a tip: listen. Hear any laughter? Laughter is one of the most telling metrics of a healthy office.

The Best Companies Don't Take Themselves Too Seriously

Cary pulled two large chairs out of their boxes and assembled them in our lounge. Satisfied with their positioning, his attention focused on the large, leftover cardboard boxes. Looking across the office and noticing an empty desk, Cary remembered that Ben, our Front-end Development Manager, was out that week on vacation. Suddenly hit by wondrous inspiration, Cary knew what he had to do.

After about a half hour, Cary stood back to admire his creation. He had fashioned a cozy cardboard cabin around Ben's desk, complete with a roof and front door.

But it didn't stop there.

Delighted by the initial effort, the team pitched in and began improvements and additions on the cabin throughout the week. A nice AstroTurf lawn sprung up. Plants, flowers, a walking path, flamingos, and a garden gnome soon joined the scene. The cardboard cabin was furnished with a chimney, windows, mailbox, and welcome mat.

As Ben returned the next Monday, we watched his reaction as he walked in and discovered his new cardboard workplace home. As we anticipated, he found the creation quite hilarious. We wondered if he would want it removed, but within a few hours, he was right at home, writing JavaScript in his cozy cabin. He loved it so much, in fact, that I think it would still be there if I didn't eventually have it removed after a couple of weeks.

Blue Compass culture takes lightheartedness very seriously. We have leaders who laugh at themselves. We have managers who can take a joke. We tease each other. You know you're in a great culture when your coworkers can tease each other and don't fear repercussions.

For some reason, there's this idea that work is supposed to be serious and difficult. Fridays are wonderful, the weekends are amazing, and Mondays are horrible, right? Songs like, "Workin' for the Weekend," "Livin' for the Weekend," "Ready for the Weekend," and "Finally Friday" only illustrate our culture's obsession with the joys of Saturday and Sunday. The secret, however, is that Monday through Friday can be just as wonderful as the weekend.

Work should be fun! Your office should be a place of joy! Your coworkers should be your friends! When your office takes itself too seriously, it's hard to experience any of these things.

What can you do? Start by not taking yourself too seriously. Don't allow yourself to be offended. Stop competing with your coworkers. Don't let the status of others threaten you. Look for reasons to laugh. Tell a joke. Do something silly. Make fun of yourself. Smile.

Recently, while walking by our office cafe, I noticed someone had brought in a few dozen cupcakes. A number of our team members were standing around, talking and enjoying the treat. Quickly, while no one was looking, I reached for a knife and cut off the top of a cupcake (the best part), took the frosting topped goodness and walked away. That's a small, random little act, but I did it because I knew it would cause a little humorous, joyful confusion. Sure enough, about five minutes later, a small commotion arose. "Who did this!?" someone exclaimed. Soon a little investigative team formed. Theories about who the guilty cupcake criminal could be were debated. It was a small act that resulted in an interesting and humorous situation. Eventually, all signs pointed to me, and I was forever labeled the cupcake-top bandit.

I won't let the inherent professionalism or assumed seriousness of the workplace stop me from creating a little fun. Neither should you. Laugh at yourself and allow others to do so as well.

Leaders are Responsible for Fostering a Joyful Workplace

I recently sat on a company culture panel at a large business conference. During the Q & A section, one of the attendees asked, "Who is responsible for maintaining a good company culture, the leader or the employee?" It's a great question.

My answer was brief: "The senior leader is responsible for the company's culture. But every employee has a part to play as well. If you're an employee who gossips then complains about the culture, you're part of the problem."

Everyone wants to be part of an organization that's full of joy. Every CEO would tell you that they desire a happy workforce. Every manager wants to manage cheerful team members. Why, then, do so few of us experience a joyful workplace?

According to a survey by The Conference Board Inc., 53 percent of Americans are currently unhappy at work.[8] That's a staggeringly depressing statistic. Over half of us don't like what we do each and every day.

The primary reason most people feel their workplace lacks joy is simple: poor leadership. If a company's leaders don't value joy, it will be difficult to find joy in the company.

Today, so many bosses are pressured to increase revenue, boost efficiency, handle unending meetings, and clear out that inbox full of 82 emails, 23 of which are high priority. It's easy for leaders to have blurred vision that can't see beyond the to-do list. There's something just as important, if not more important, than the daily tasks: being positive and lighthearted.

The best leaders have fun. They not only allow surprises, but they plan one themselves every once and a while. They take time to chat with others. They value relationships with team members more than to-do lists.

The best leaders don't just allow fun; they cause it.

If you're a leader, you must spend a significant amount of your time purposefully enhancing the environment of the organization. Author Scott Berkun conveyed this sentiment well when he wrote, "Every CEO is, in fact, a Chief Cultural Officer. The terrifying thing is it's the CEO's actual behavior, not their speeches or the list of values they have put up on posters, that defines what the culture is."

As I mentioned in chapter two, I've come to realize that my number one responsibility as CEO of a company is actually pretty simple: to know our values and make them known. It took me years to realize that the most valuable thing I can contribute to my team is the fostering of a great culture.

Our company has grown significantly since our inception in 2007. Naturally, I've interviewed hundreds of people over the years and believe it or not, I've been pranked many times during those interviews.

Our large conference room has a wall made entirely of glass, and typically interviewees sit with their backs to this wall. Therefore, the interviewer can easily see what's behind the interviewee.

Years ago, people started trying to make the interviewer laugh, unbeknownst to the interviewee. It started innocently, with team members making funny faces or pushing each other around on chairs. Things escalated quickly, however. Recently, I've witnessed a half dozen people carry my business partner across the room, a developer running and sliding as if he was stealing second base and five team members put on wigs and dance to a country song.

Is this professional behavior? Perhaps not. But I never put a stop to it. Why? Because this is who we are. We're silly. We're wild. We choose joy.

But what if the interviewee happens to turn around and witness these shenanigans (which does occasionally happen)? Then at least they know who we are. If they don't like a culture like ours, it's better they find out sooner rather than later.

Occasionally, we even use these office hijinks as an interview tool. Recently we interviewed an individual that I was particularly concerned about. She had fantastic experience and skills that we needed, but there was a problem. She was very solemn and a bit negative. During our interview, she barely expressed any emotions, didn't smile and voiced a few complaints about her current employer. I felt concerned she wouldn't be able to handle our humorous office culture. Was I being too picky, or was my concern warranted?

We devised a little test. In the middle of her next interview, two of our team members squeezed into the cart that we use to move food and drinks around while another sat on top. A fourth team member happily pushed them through our entryway, just outside our main conference room. We made sure they were loud enough to get the interviewee's attention. She turned around, witnessed the odd sight, and turned back to the interview, thoroughly unimpressed. There's nothing wrong with her reaction, but she wasn't right for our culture.

As a leader, you're responsible for encouraging an authentic culture. You can't mandate positivity. You must genuinely encourage it and participate in it yourself.

Stop focusing only on that to-do list. Your behaviors are more important than clearing out your inbox.

The Power of Positive, Thoughtful Surprises

If you're looking to bring more moments of joy into your office, there's one ingredient that will make your efforts more effective: surprise. When you plan something fun and make it unexpected, it enhances the experience.

Recently, a spontaneous Oreo taste-testing event sprung up in our office. I brought about 10 packs of various Oreos to the office and set them out in our cafe. I cut a few pieces of paper, set out a pen, and wrote a note that simply said, "vote for your favorite."

Small, surprise moments like this are powerful. These out-of-the-ordinary events boost morale not just because they are fun but because they are a pleasant surprise. They get team members together, break up the daily routine, and create moments of bonding. It required an incredibly small amount of time and budget to set up, and our team appreciated the experience (and for those keeping track, Marshmallow Chocolate Oreos were crowned the tastiest, though I'm confident Carrot Cake Oreos are the best).

Of course, not every spontaneous moment of fun lands the way you want it. I also recently purchased a few cricket energy bars and set them in our cafe. With actual crickets as the main ingredient, these bars are supposedly tasty and full of protein. While they did get the office talking, only three people were brave enough to try the snacks. It didn't quite bring the team together like I had hoped (you win some, you lose some).

When we look for opportunities to encourage and appreciate without warning, powerful things happen. A positive, unexpected surprise can ignite feelings of gratitude in people.

In his book, *The Best Place to Work*, Ron Friedman explains that unexpected pleasures deliver a bigger thrill. "When something surprising happens, our brains automatically pay closer attention, lending unexpected events a greater emotional weight. We're motivated to make sense of events we haven't predicted and devote more mental energy to thinking about them after they occur. In this way, surprises provide an emotional exclamation point, enhancing the impact of any event, good or bad."

While our team frequently eats lunch together, our favorite lunches are monthly birthday/anniversary lunches. We bring a meal into our cafe, eat together, then celebrate the birthdays and work anniversaries of the month. If a new team member is with us, we'll have each person introduce the team member to their left and share an interesting fact or two about him or her.

The most well-received part of the lunch, however, is the game we play. We always create an original game that awards the winning person or team with a prize, such as a gift card. For instance, we once played "Name that Office Object," in which we simply took close-up photos of various things around the office and then presented them on a slide deck. Another game is "Epic Pictionary," in which, the day before, we give a notecard with a unique sentence to all team members. Then we show each drawing on a slide and challenge each team member to guess what sentence generated that drawing.

At one birthday/anniversary lunch, I hadn't had time to come up with a game but didn't want to omit the best part of the lunch. Off the top of my head, I said, "For today's game, we're playing hide and seek." Surprisingly, this simple idea went over extremely well. It was as if I had announced all team members were receiving a ten-thousand-dollar bonus. The entire team was ecstatic at the proposition.

Everyone split up into teams, with one person from each team hiding from our CFO. I was impressed with the creativity employed to select hiding places. Brooke removed the contents and shelves of one of our refrigerators, allowing Stephanie to hide inside (a true display of her team-first attitude, as Stephanie has claustrophobia). David somehow climbed up in the ceiling rafters, won the game, and barely made it down alive.

In short, the game was a big hit. But why was such a simple child's game so successful in a modern, professional office filled with adults? Because of our first value: positivity! When we first began thinking about establishing our values, we knew that fun and positivity were essential elements we always wanted in our work environment. Our first value has helped us never forget not to take ourselves too seriously and to show joy at work.

In chapter three, I shared how we celebrated Employee Appreciation Day by bringing a party bus to the office and touring the city together. While this gesture was a wonderful experience, what made it even more impactful was that it was totally unexpected. We were very purposeful in keeping this experience quiet as we wanted it to be a surprise.

I regularly stop at a coffee shop on the way to work and buy a coffee for a team member. As I mentioned, we have a list of every employee's favorite things, including coffee, making it easy for me to quickly check which type of coffee to buy. I'm always one of the first to arrive in the office, so I'll place the drink on the team member's desk with a post-it note on which I'll include a quick message. "You are awesome - thanks for being part of this team," for instance.

It's a nice thing to do, but what enhances this gesture is the surprise. I will never tell the team member that coffee is waiting for them. Occasionally, the team member will already have brought a coffee to work, making my gift technically unnecessary. Yet the gesture is still greatly appreciated, much because of the surprise.

Ideas for Adding Joy to Your Culture

Remember, the best way to get others to engage in a behavior is to do it yourself. Step away from email and have a little fun yourself. Choose joy. Here are a few ideas for adding joy to your workplace (and of course, each is better if it's unexpected):

- Play company trivia over lunch and give out gift cards to the winners.
- Have a nerf gun fight in the office.
- Write a random thank you note to a team member. Leave it on his desk before he arrives at work or send it to him in the mail.
- Hire a quartet to sing for someone's birthday.
- Have a "bring your dog to work" day.
- Bring a team member's favorite coffee to work and leave it on her desk before she arrives.
- Bake cookies.
- Send a Grubhub or DoorDash gift card to each team member.

- For Mothers' Day, have each team member's mom record a message about what her son or daughter was like as a child.
- Jump out and scare a coworker (who enjoys surprises).
- Have a "cereal day," in which each team member is encouraged to bring his or her favorite breakfast food for a cereal potluck.
- Have an office or Internet scavenger hunt.
- Hold a "wine and cheese" o'clock event.
- Have a "Get to know _____ (insert team member's name here)" 15-minute break in the middle of the day during which each person asks that team member a question.
- Put a 1,000 piece puzzle out in a community space and watch as team members slowly put it together little by little over the next few days.
- Have a "team spirit day," in which everyone is encouraged to wear their favorite sports team's apparel.
- Film a humorous video in which you (nicely) make fun of the boss or department manager and watch it together as a team.
- Do a half-day service project in the community as a company or department.
- Have an office awards show in which you give out "the most outgoing in the morning award, the best dressed awards, the most likely to laugh during a meeting award," etc.

MAJOR TAKEAWAYS

- Regular doses of small bits of fun lead to a strong and joyful company culture.

- You can't have a truly successful team without strong relationships. You can't have strong relationships without bonding. And one of the best ways to bond is to have fun together.
- The best office cultures are filled with people who don't take themselves too seriously.
- The best leaders don't just allow fun; they create it.
- When you plan something fun and make it unexpected, it enhances the experience.

CHAPTER 5

COMPANY CULTURE KEY #4: CONSTANT CONNECTION

"The business of business is relationships; the business of life is human connection." - Robin S. Sharma

Our digital marketing workload was finally growing. After years of going to conferences, reading blog articles, and growing our expertise, my dream of having a thriving digital marketing department was coming to life. Clients were signing up for search engine optimization, social media campaigns and user-experience improvements for their websites. We were getting busy and we needed to hire.

At the time, our Digital Marketing Department consisted of just four people (a manager, a strategist, and two associates) and we needed another associate. I knew the addition of another digital marketer would significantly impact the dynamic of the small team. Additionally, I knew that adding a new employee can sometimes feel a little threatening to others. When someone is added to your team with the same job title as yours, it can cause you to wonder if your future growth opportunities have changed.

Since we were hiring a new Digital Marketing Associate, I decided to let our current two associates know what we were planning and ensure them that this didn't change their importance and opportunities.

It seemed like a good idea, and I didn't think much of it at the time. Fast-forward seven years. I was having a conversation with Katrina, our Digital Marketing Director. While we were discussing potential hiring prospects, she mentioned how much it meant to her when, seven years ago, I communicated our hiring plans and assured her we still valued her. She was one of those associates.

Relationships Matter Even More Than Billable Hours

Here's a simple but valuable insight: the more you spend time with someone the more that person trusts you.

I'm a big believer in having coffees and lunches with others. I'm happy to meet anyone at a coffee shop or restaurant. I don't think I've ever said no to such a request. A soon-to-be college graduate recently reached out to me, asking to have coffee. I agreed and met him at a coffee shop. We had a nice conversation. I asked questions about his major, interests, and professional aspirations. At the end of the conversation, I knew more about him, saw his perspective, and appreciated him more than before the coffee. A professional connection began, and today he works at Blue Compass.

Consider what happens when you have coffee or lunch with a friend or coworker. Nine times out of 10, you walk away liking that person a little more. The reason is simple. The more time you spend with someone, the more you hear his side of things. The more you learn about his life, his desires, struggles and aspirations. Spending time with someone builds empathy. Want someone to like you more? Spend quality time with that person. Time together grows relationships.

Tom Clegg, President and founder of Clegg Consulting, says, "Disfunction draws all of its power from the silence in which it dwells." Indeed, problems arise when conversations aren't happening. It's a leader's job to break the silence and get to the right conversation. Those who build relationships in the workplace are building walls of protection against problems.

If you want an incredible work environment, you've got to take the time to focus on something other than "business." Take time to connect with people. Regardless of your role, getting to know your coworkers is always worth the effort.

I've read numerous books that explain the importance of productive meetings. Get to the point. Be efficient. Stop wasting time with chit-chat. But I don't buy it. At Blue Compass, our meetings nearly always start with five to ten minutes of stories, teasing, questions, and conversation. I've never shut this down because building relationships with one another is just as important as the purpose of our meetings.

Can this principle be overdone? Of course. I'm sure we're occasionally guilty of too much conversation. It's critical to be efficient and get real work done but not at the expense of connecting with your team members.

Leaders who genuinely care about their team members are purposeful about building trust. "Engendering a culture of trust also does wonders," according to Patrick Campbell, Co-founder and CEO of ProfitWell. "This is because, even if you have a heated argument, as long as you keep in the back of your mind that the people you're arguing with do have the best in mind for the company and wider team, you'll always be able to make it to the end and remain friendly."

Former CEO of Xerox Corporation Ann M. Mulcahy summed up the incredible value of leaders who truly care for their team members by saying, "Employees who believe that management is concerned about them as a whole person — not just an employee — are more productive, more satisfied, more fulfilled. Satisfied employees mean satisfied customers, which leads to profitability."

A recent Harvard Business Review survey reveals 58 percent of people say they trust strangers more than their own boss.[9] Why does our society generally consider bosses to be difficult and overbearing? I believe it's because most bosses focus too much on the numbers and not enough on the people. There's a lot of pressure put on business leaders to focus on the metrics. Companies must continually be growing their profits, capabilities, and efficiencies. But if our leaders will take the time to slow down and listen to their team, ask questions, understand the people and connect, amazing things can happen.

The surprising secret is that the best way to grow the bottom line is to stop focusing entirely on growing the bottom line and focus more on the people.

The Power of Small Talk

Have you ever met someone who can walk up to anyone and create an engaging conversation? Laura, our VP of Operations, is one such person. I've worked with her for many years and have always been amazed at her ability to connect with our team members. She's fantastic at listening, asking questions and chatting with anyone. With simple questions like, "How was your weekend?" and, "How are you doing today?", she starts amazing conversations that make us all feel important and cared for.

One of the ways to connect with your team members is to chat with them. I'm a fairly outgoing person, but sometimes I hesitate to do this. It's easy to focus on your to-do list and let people take care of themselves. But engaging in small talk is an important way to connect with your team.

Yet "small talk" seems to have a negative connotation. It's often viewed as a superfluous string of shallow words that have no real value.

While small talk can be shallow, it still has great value. It's a way to acknowledge someone and show them you care enough to interact. Additionally, small talk is the doorway to great conversation.

As American philosopher William James once said, "Conversation does flourish, and society is refreshing... whenever people take the brakes off their hearts, and let their tongues wag as automatically and irresponsibly as they will." Opening up and talking to a colleague will leave both of you in a better relationship.

In his book, *How to Have Confidence and Power in Dealing with People*, Les Giblin states that, "Small talk is necessary to get the wheels turning. Once you realize this and stop being afraid of being dull, you will find that you too can start a conversation, even with a perfect stranger, and you may be surprised to find that, in many cases, you are saying clever and interesting things—only because you aren't trying to."

Your professional reputation is not on the line. Take the pressure off yourself. Don't feel like your conversation has to be brilliant or life-changing. Just make small talk, and you'll both be better for it.

Having a good conversation isn't about saying clever, meaningful, memorable things. It's about caring enough for the other person to listen and share a few of your own thoughts.

The Best Leaders are Listeners

Years ago, when we were building out our current office, we made an unusual decision: Blue Compass would have no doors.

Seriously, no doors? Of course we do have doors allowing people in and out of the office, on conference rooms and restrooms (thankfully), but every other room simply features an open doorway. Why? Because we don't just want to have an open-door policy, we want a no-door policy. Our leadership team members make it clear that they are always available to listen. Nothing separates us from the rest of the team.

One of the most effective ways your leadership team can foster a positive culture is to make it clear that they are always willing to listen.

Your team members want to know they can be heard if they have something to say. They want to know you'll listen if they speak. Many managers, however, struggle to truly listen.

Have you ever been in a conversation with a person and found yourself preparing a response in your head while you zone out and miss what the other person is actually saying? It's something we're all likely guilty of. As Proverbs 18:2 states, "A fool takes no pleasure in understanding, but only in expressing his opinion."

"The biggest communication problem is we do not listen to understand. We listen to reply." This remark was made by author and businessman Stephen Covey and conveys one of the most important principles anyone who interacts with people should know: truly listening to others is absolutely essential.

When someone is talking to you, have the disciple to actively listen. Don't interrupt. Don't worry about getting your point across. Ask clarifying questions so that you fully understand the other person. Doing so will not only give you insight and help you empathize but will create a positive bond between the two of you. People love people who listen. Have the confidence to hear the other's thoughts before expressing your own.

As Les Giblin states, "Good human relations consist of two-way communication. It's give and take, action and response. If you don't know what the other fellow wants, how he really feels about a situation, what his own peculiar needs are, you are out of touch with him. And if you can't touch him, you can't move him. Unless you know what he wants, and how he feels, you are completely in the dark concerning his position."

Make it clear that you are an active listener. When employees realize they work for an organization that values their voice, they will feel safe and be less likely to leave.

The Power of One-on-one Meetings

One of the best practices we've implemented over the years is regular one-on-one meetings with each team member. At a regular cadence (typically once every week or every two weeks), each team member receives an individual meeting with their manager. It's simply a time to check in and see how everything is going with the team members. The manager will ask questions like:

- How are you doing?
- What's working well?
- What's your biggest struggle right now?
- How can we better support you?

It's also a time to give feedback, guidance, and share any necessary updates.

The constant connection that these meetings create is fantastic. This practice allows both team members and managers to understand one another, feel heard, and grow a positive relationship.

While I believe these meetings can greatly benefit any organization, they have to be handled in the right way. If you implement a similar practice, your managers must be purposeful about treating these meetings as an important opportunity both for the employee and the company. One-on-ones must not be viewed as an ongoing chore.

In one of her past work experiences, my wife was supposed to have regular one-on-ones with her manager. While she saw these meetings as a valuable opportunity to ask questions and share her viewpoint, her manager didn't see things the same way. She once waited for 15 minutes for him to arrive at their one-on-one. When he finally appeared, he blurted, "Do you even have anything to talk to me about? I'm super busy today." Clearly, this was a horrible approach that ruptured the relationship. These meetings must be taken seriously, especially by the manager.

How Transparency Improves Culture

One of the most important aspects of constant connection is transparency. Your organization must build trust with employees to be successful, but that's difficult to do when it doesn't share information. People don't want to work for a company that appears to keep secrets.

Many years ago, transparency in the workplace wasn't expected. Today's youngest workers, however, deeply desire to know what's going on. They are more likely than the members of any other generation to share salary information with their coworkers, which exemplifies their desire for transparency in the workplace and demonstrates how they create transparency where it does not already exist.[10]

Just a few hours before the writing of this section, I led a team meeting in which we showed our financials from the last quarter. We displayed how many clients paid us and how much income came from web development, digital marketing, website hosting, and our conference center. This is a common practice for us; we're very transparent with our financials. It takes minimal effort for any Blue Compass team member to understand exactly where we sit financially. That's not always comfortable for me, but I believe the team appreciates the information and trusts us more because of it.

Many businesses are hesitant to make this move as they fear employees may consider jumping ship if financials are bad. Or, if things are good, they may expect a large raise or bonus. As the CEO of our company, I absolutely understand that. But the thing is, your team members can make those assessments based on many factors, not just your financials. Being transparent with your numbers builds trust with your team and allows you to articulate the narrative. We've done this for years, and I've not experienced any negatives from doing so.

Is it essential that you share all your financials with your team? Of course not. Each company is different. This is something that works well for us. The point is, being transparent builds rapport with your employees.

In addition to sharing finances, we also use our team meetings to update the team on many other aspects of our company. The latest projects we've won, concerns about the business, victories and successes, upcoming events, hiring needs, etc. If you're in a position of leadership, it's easy to assume your employees are in the know, but it's likely they are uninformed in comparison with you.

Use your company meetings, department meetings, and one-on-one meetings to share information. Even if you feel most people already know the happenings around the office, share anyway. I've never heard a professional complain about overcommunication.

The Best Leaders Show Appropriate Vulnerability

All Blue Compass team members undergo an annual review, including myself. At the end of each year, I reflect on the year and fill out our annual review form, just like everyone else on our team. I'm critical of myself and honest with my feedback. I discuss areas of needed improvement but also share my successes from the year.

Once I've completed the form, I email my review out to the team and invite their feedback. Everyone on our team, from interns to VPs, can read about my personal successes and failures from the year, as well as my goals and areas of improvement for the coming year.

Sharing your vulnerabilities with others can truly be difficult. Conversely, seeking the approval of others is natural. We all crave the acceptance of others and desire to impress our peers. Nowhere is this more true than in the workplace, where others' perception of us impacts not only our daily experience but our financial standing. This is just as true in the c-suite, if not more so, as in the rest of the organization. While we often don't perceive their need for acceptance, the truth is that most bosses deeply desire to impress the team.

As strange as it may sound, revealing your vulnerabilities is one of the best ways to connect with your team members, especially if you are in a position of leadership. As leadership and management coach Perry Holley says, "Being vulnerable as a leader is about being open with others about your need for help, admitting you do not have all the answers, and accepting you are not the answer to every problem."[11]

While showing vulnerability is often associated with weakness, it's actually the opposite. Being vulnerable with your team members is a strength that requires courage. It's natural for us to want to hide our faults and emphasize our successes but our team members already know many of our weaknesses. Being open and honest about your struggles is more authentic than hiding them. Your peers will perceive you as more honest and trustworthy.

Don't be mistaken, however. Being professionally vulnerable doesn't mean oversharing every fault and struggle. As Holley says, "I do NOT confess every weakness and mistake, but I open myself to sharing the challenges and struggles relevant to our journey together." We've all seen people who overshare both in person and on social media. Pouring out your struggles and complaints to anyone who will listen is not professional vulnerability. It's negativity.

Company Cliques Create Catastrophic Carnage

My wife, Melíssa, once worked at a corporation where she was put in charge of a team in one region, while another VP led the same type of team in another region. The two teams shared no projects and had little interaction, yet immediately after Melíssa's assignment to this position, the VP of the other region began to focus negatively on Melíssa's team. She was constantly checking in on their progress. She became upset when her team members interacted with Melíssa, and she complained when Melíssa planned a team outing with her team because it made her feel bad that she hadn't planned one with hers.

This woman spent a tremendous amount of energy being threatened by a team that had no direct impact on her team, despite both teams being part of the same company! Think how much more productive and happy she would have been if she had simply kept her focus on serving her team and clients.

Pride produces jealousy, and jealousy produces opposition. One of the worst forms of opposition in the professional world is workplace cliques. When a few people intentionally or unintentionally form a group that views others as opposition, trouble is on the horizon.

I'm surprised by how little attention this subject receives. Workplace cliques are so common I think most of us have just come to accept them as a way of life. Cliques exist in elementary school, middle school, high school, and college. Of course, they're going to exist in the office, right?

Workplace cliques divide teams. When these divisions exist in your organization, employees will expend energy trying to deal with the clique. They will be on the defensive. They will look for faults in other groups. They will focus on the success of their group more than the success of the company.

Imagine a Major League Baseball team forming cliques. The outfielders stick together and are threatened by the other players. The infielders believe they're the best and deserve more credit. The pitcher and catcher can't believe the rest of the team gets paid as well as they do. Trust and camaraderie are in short supply. Clearly, this team is doomed to failure with no hope of a championship, let alone a winning record.

Workplace cliques form between like-minded people who have something in common. These can be a number of things, such as personality types, tenure at the company, or the location at which they work. The most common type I've seen, however, is the infamous department clique. In my experience, companies that have rival departments are especially doomed.

Recently, one of our developers and one of our digital marketers took the time to create a new tool to make the setup of Google Analytics preferences and profiles more efficient. The tool will potentially save us hours of work on new digital marketing projects. I had no idea this tool was being built but was very pleased to see these two team members from different departments use their free time to work together to improve our process.

When people ask me what sets Blue Compass apart from our competitors, one of the things I cite is how well our departments work together. I've seen many organizations that struggle in this area. It's not uncommon for a marketing department to butt heads with IT, for instance. Incredible things can happen, however, when departments are aligned.

Do cliques exist in your organization? My guess is you can easily think of a few right now, but there may be some you don't perceive. A few signs of work cliques include:

- Team members who spend excessive time together, rarely interacting with others
- Team members who regularly exclude others
- Team members who gossip about others
- Team members who talk negatively about others
- Team members who are excessively competitive with other internal groups

The reality is very simply: you cannot have a good culture when groups of employees view each other as the enemy. Your company must discourage all workplace cliques.

But how?

First, tell your team how important it is that everyone supports each other. Internal messaging from your CEO, VPs, managers, etc., should focus on the importance of togetherness. Seek opportunities to allow someone from one department to publicly compliment other departments. Praise those who work well with other groups. Use meetings, emails, internal chat, newsletters, etc., to advance this messaging.

Create opportunities for employees to get together and bond with team members that are outside of their normal bubble. For instance, we occasionally have team lunches in which we assign groups of a half dozen or so team members to eat together and specifically choose people who don't work together directly. Each group gets to pick a restaurant from which we order lunch and are given a number of entertaining questions to answer together.

It may be necessary to have direct conversations with team members who are especially opposed to other groups in the office. Be clear that everyone in your organization is on the same team. Share clear expectations that everyone is supportive and positive towards other departments. Discuss this with employees in regular one-on-one meetings.

Perhaps the most important thing you can personally do to discourage internal divisions in your company is to never publicly favor one group of employees over another. Model the behavior you want from others.

MAJOR TAKEAWAYS

- To build trust with team members, leaders must show they truly care through genuine, ongoing conversations.
- Those who build relationships in the workplace are building walls of protection against problems.
- One of the most effective ways your leadership can foster a positive culture is make it clear that they are always willing to listen.
- Regular one-on-one meetings allow both team members and managers to understand one another, feel heard and grow a positive relationship.

- People don't want to work for a company that appears to keep secrets
- Transparency builds rapport with employees.
- Leaders who are open their struggles are perceived as more honest and trustworthy.
- One of the worst threats to positive company culture are workplace cliques.

CHAPTER 6
COMPANY CULTURE KEY #5: GENUINE GROWTH

"The important thing is that we must be constantly moving forward… and our growth should never end." - Og Mandino

Many years ago, not long after I became a leader, a few of my team members and I flew across the country to attend a marketing conference in New Orleans. While walking around the main floor in between sessions, I noticed a group of three employees and their boss manning a booth. While the employees were busy interacting with passersby and demoing their product, the boss sat off to the side on her phone.

I kept an eye on them each time I passed by the conference floor, only to notice the same scenario. The boss continued to sit nearby on her phone, while the employees worked on their own.

At the end of the conference, we said our goodbyes, grabbed our swag bags and drove to the airport. As we boarded our plane, I noticed the boss of this company happened to be on the same plane, seated in first class. As my team and I made our way past first class, we saw her employees huddled together in the back. They were literally sitting in the very last row of the plane.

This experience made a huge impact on me. It taught me that true leaders don't sit ahead of their team, they sit with their team. It's a lesson that's driven much of my career and my passion for positive company culture. In many ways, it helped inspire this book.

Great leaders strive to improve so that they can better serve their team. As pastor and leadership expert Craig Groeschel says, "Everyone wins when leaders get better." Great company culture requires great leaders.

It's not just leaders who must continually improve, however. Everyone at your organization must get better. In fact, most people won't be truly happy at a company unless they have the opportunity to develop their skills, knowledge, and career. A truly great company culture allows team members to grow.

There's Little Happiness Without Growth

Whether we realize it or not, each of us desires to get better. Thankfully, personal development can help us realize our dreams and improve our quality of life. Learning the right skills can allow us to thrive in any scenario and can provide great contentment. I've found personal development to be a large source of happiness in my life.

One of the questions I ask in interviews is, "Imagine you worked here for one year and decided this is absolutely the best job you've ever had. What would make you feel that way?" The majority of the time, the interviewees give a response such as, "I grew professionally and made great relationships with the team and clients." Indeed, most professionals recognize the value of growing their abilities and feel it's important to keep getting better.

Of course the personal growth of your team members isn't just beneficial for them, it's beneficial for your organization as well. "Better results come from being a better person," motivational speaker and leadership expert Jim Rohn once said. "The big challenge is to become all that you have the possibility of becoming. You cannot believe what it does to the human spirit to maximize your human potential and stretch yourself to the limit." Learning can increase motivation, improve confidence, boost creativity, and help provide a sense of direction. It brings incredibly positive outcomes for both the employee and the company.

At Blue Compass, we're big believers in continual growth, both for our team members and our company. As mentioned in chapter two, one of our five value statements is: "We grow our expertise."

Your organization may excel at Incredible Culture Keys 1 through 4, but if you don't have an environment that allows team members to experience genuine growth, you'll still struggle to retain the best talent. In my experience, this is especially true with young employees. Younger people seem especially interested in learning and growth.

Creating a Culture of Gratifying Growth

At the beginning of each of our team meetings, we hold a learning session. I usually lead these sessions, but often we'll be joined by a guest speaker, or we'll watch a video together. Over the past few months, we've covered topics like positivity, failure, stress, responsibility, and happiness. Our team members always seem to appreciate these sessions. A few years ago, I led a session on the value of assuming the best in every situation. It made a significant impact, and still today team members will occasionally remind each other to "assume the best."

Great companies focus on regular learning opportunities for their team members. This is a growing trend for many organizations these days. Airbnb, for instance, uses regular "Fireside Chats" to help its team grow and learn. These internal events feature external speakers who share their insights on a certain topic. Airbnb says, "From CEOs to musicians, these leaders always have something invaluable to teach us."[12]

Etsy uses a regular learning program called "Etsy School" to allow employees to both teach and learn in classes on topics like navigating difficult conversations. The Etsy Learning and Development team helps people find a focus for their career development.[13]

Your company doesn't need to adopt high-profile speakers or extensive classes to help your employees develop. Here are a few inexpensive and relatively simple things we've done to include regular learning opportunities that may work for you:

- **Department Learning Meetings** - All our departments have regular meetings at which team members are encouraged to bring and share one thing they've learned since the last meeting. This is a very simple and effective way to encourage others to learn and start great conversations.

- **Lunch 'n' Learns** - At these occasional lunches, we choose a topic relevant to everyone, provide lunch, and have a team member or two teach the group. The food and setting keep everything casual and lead to great questions. It's an effective way to get your entire team or department in the learning spirit together.

- **Weekly Recap Email** - At the end of each week, one of the members of our Digital Marketing Department sends a weekly recap email that shares what's happened in the world of SEO, Google, Twitter, online ads, etc. This is a fantastic value to our team members, and it allows all of us to get caught up on what's going on in our industry in a short amount of time. Consider assigning a different team member each week to spend a half-hour researching what's new and relevant in your industry and sharing it internally via email.

- **Webinars** - Organizations or thought leaders in most industries offer free or low-cost webinars that can provide great value. We regularly find a good webinar and schedule time for a few team members to watch it together. If the webinar was especially helpful, we'll schedule another meeting for the attendees to share their notes with the rest of the team or department.

- **Online Classes** - Occasionally, there's a specific subject that requires in-depth research and study. In these cases, we may sign a team member up for an online class. This is especially common with some of the programming and security that affect our development team.

- **Conferences** - While they can be expensive and take your team members away from work for a number of days, in-person conferences can be one of the best learning opportunities available. We've received fantastic value from these over the years. When sending your team members to a conference, schedule time for them to assemble their notes afterward and teach their department the essential takeaways.

- **Book Clubs** - One of my favorite ways to learn, "Blue Compass Book Clubs," are always fantastic experiences. We select a good book and schedule regular meetings to discuss a chapter or two at a time. This can be good for a department to read together, just an employee and a manager, or even an entire company.

Great Feedback Leads to Great Development

The quality of a person's manager is one of the greatest indicators of how well that person can professionally develop. One of the most significant ways managers can influence the growth of their reports is through honest, positive evaluations of their actions. Employees cannot experience significant professional growth if they're not receiving quality feedback and guidance.

As the saying goes, "people don't leave bad jobs, they leave bad bosses." If someone reports to you, it's essential that you genuinely care for that person and regularly connect with her (as discussed in chapter five). You must truly desire for that person to grow and succeed (if you don't, a managerial role isn't for you). One of the most important things you can do is provide honest, helpful feedback.

The problem, however, is that many managers struggle to give good guidance. This is the case for many reasons, but there are two main culprits. One, managers are often very busy with their own work and it's difficult to put time and energy into considering the development of those in their care. Two, giving honest feedback can be uncomfortable and it's easy to avoid.

Employees will have difficulty growing if their company's management or leadership is unable to provide real feedback and have tough conversations when necessary. As Tom Clegg says, "Leaders are limited by the conversations they don't have."

If you're a leader, realize that whether it's in your job description or not, your purpose is to allow others to grow and flourish. Have the boldness and kindness to offer both praise and correction. Correcting someone can be difficult, but it's actually a very kind action. Showing someone the error of his ways and guiding him down a more positive path is truly a gracious act.

Whether you see your direct report doing something positive or negative, provide helpful feedback quickly. Feedback must be specific, contain a clear expectation of what can be improved, and must be given with kindness. As Frank A. Clark once said, "Criticism, like rain, should be gentle enough to nourish a man's growth without destroying his roots." Don't save your thoughts and guidance for months. The goal is to help the other person get better. Giving feedback on something that happened weeks ago will have a much less significant impact since the occurrence is no longer timely. "Make feedback normal. Not a performance review," says executive coach Ed Batista.

Additionally, feedback should generally be given in private. Correction feels more like punishment when others are privy to it.

If you want to grow in your career, seek feedback. Consider it. Accept it. And perhaps most importantly, don't allow yourself to be insulted by it.

Pave a Path of Career Growth

While personal development for employees should clearly be a focus for organizations, a career path for each employee is also crucial. These days, most professionals actively seek opportunities to be promoted and gain new job titles. If your organization is perceived as a place where there's no opportunity for career advancement, employees will eventually seek greener pastures.

People and organizations are complex. The subject of when and how to promote employees is certainly a complicated one that can't fully be covered in this chapter alone. Here are a few ways, however, that we carve a career path for our team members and help them visualize the opportunities ahead.

First, discuss the career path. Be open to discussing what the employee's future at the organization looks like. Sometimes employers purposely avoid this subject because they don't want to get the employee too focused on a promotion or a raise, but facing the subject directly is the best approach.

We've found that the best way to do this is to be aware of our team members' passions. The ideal career direction for an employee is the direction of his passion, so long as it helps the company. A few times a year, check in on what that team member enjoys doing the most and what he is feeling most passionate about. Then talk with him about what opportunities may be in that area. For instance, if we have a team member who shares that he is passionate about reaching people with local search engine optimization, this gives both us and him a good idea of where his future may lie within the company.

Once an employee is providing great value for the company and is approaching the point where he is ready to move on to a new role, begin talking more about that next step and provide a specific checklist of things you need to see from him before he will be promoted (if necessary). If a promotion is going to eventually happen, it should be planned and purposeful, with clear expectations. The right promotion at the right time will be an immense blessing to both the employee and the company. A poorly planned promotion, however, can pull both parties down to the depths of conflict and misery.

Discussing future growth opportunities with an employee can be more difficult in a smaller organization. In a large corporation, there are typically numerous career paths and clear roads to different job titles. In a small organization, however, there's not necessarily such a clear path. If your company only has 10 people, there may not be an obvious promotion opportunity.

One of the advantages a small business has, however, is freedom and flexibility. In most cases, a small business can restructure, create new roles, and form new departments without the complications and red tape corporations face. Since Blue Compass isn't a mega-corporation, we'll occasionally share that we simply aren't yet sure what role is the next step for a team member, but we're open to creating a new role or opportunity for that team member in the future, as long as it makes sense for our business.

The Opportunities and Dangers of the All-Important Job Title

For better or worse, there's a significant focus on titles in the modern workplace. While titles have always been important to people, today's younger workers seem especially focused on them.

Don't be dismissive of employees' titles. It can be advantageous for both the employee and the manager to consider the future and have a new job title in mind for that employee to work towards. However, resist the urge to put too much of a focus on titles.

Job titles are emphasized too heavily in our society. As novelist Anthony Trollope said, "The love of titles is common to all men." Unfortunately in the last half-century, our jobs have become our identities. For many, job titles are sources of pride and ego. That's regrettable because people are much more than their jobs. Your title does not define you. As Neil deGrasse Tyson says, "if you need to invoke your academic pedigree or job title for people to believe what you say, then you need a better argument."

When do people most often seek a new, loftier job title? When their peers receive one. Comparing yourself with someone else nearly always leads to unhappiness. It's much more beneficial to compare yourself with your past self. We inspire our team to compete with themselves, not their team members.

Encourage your team members to embrace new responsibilities and opportunities over job titles. Receiving a new responsibility at work can be an incredible chance for an employee to grow and increase her influence. You don't have to change someone's job title to provide her with more authority and opportunity.

Remember, your title doesn't make you a leader, your actions do. Emphasize responsibilities over titles. You don't need a title to have influence.

MAJOR TAKEAWAYS

- Great culture requires great leaders.

- Nearly all professionals desire to grow their skills and capabilities.
- Organizations lacking an environment that allows team members to experience gratifying growth will struggle to retain the best talent.
- Present your team with regular learning opportunities such as lunch 'n' learns, book clubs, webinars, and conferences.
- The quality of a person's manager is one of the greatest indicators to how well that person can professionally develop.
- Employees cannot experience significant professional growth if they're not receiving quality feedback and guidance.
- Have at least a general plan for the career path of each employee.
- While job titles are important, encourage your team members to embrace new responsibilities and opportunities over job titles.

CHAPTER 7
HOW TO HIRE PEOPLE WHO WILL FUEL A POSITIVE CULTURE

"Hire people who are smarter than you are—whose talents surpass yours—and give them opportunities for growth. It's the smart thing to do and it is a sign of high personal humility." - Bruna Martinuzzi

As Blue Compass continued to grow, more projects were flowing in and we were in desperate need of a new project manager. We set up a series of interviews with promising talent and the interviews began.

One young woman seemed especially promising. She was pleasant, well-spoken, and seemed very organized. As the interview ended, she rose and exited our conference room. We walked into the entryway, shook hands and I promised her we would be in touch within a week. She smiled, thanked me, turned and walked directly into the glass door. The good news is that we have a very nice office with impeccably clean, dust and fingerprint-free glass doors. The bad news is that they are apparently near-invisible.

She staggered back, stunned. A bit shocked and surprised, I didn't know what to say. Should I run to her aid and ensure she's okay?

Should I try to save her pride and act as if I didn't notice? Before I could decide she rushed out the door and disappeared. My gaze returned to the door where I could see a large makeup smudge from where her forehead impacted the glass.

That was the last time we saw the young lady, who didn't return our correspondences after that fateful day with the spotless glass door.

I've interviewed hundreds of people for jobs and have had some interesting interviews over the years. Once a guy who wanted a job sent me a trash can to get my attention (did not hire him). One interviewee detailed how lazy she could be (did not hire her). Another fellow showed us a photo of himself posing for a bodybuilding competition in a Speedo during the interview (you guessed it, we did not hire him).

Perhaps nothing impacts your company culture more than the people who comprise it. The individuals who join your department or company must be the right cultural fit. There's no more important qualification. As Jessica Herrin, founder of Stella & Dot says, "Shaping your culture is more than half done when you hire your team."

The Right Type of People to Hire

There are a wealth of people out there. How can you select team members who will be positive, supportive and help contribute to enjoyable workdays?

Somehow over the years, the professional world has decided to reduce a person's perceived value to an organization to a list of past jobs on a piece of paper. A professional's skills and experience are indeed important. Clearly, you must hire people who have the expertise to bring value to your operations, sales and clients. But a resume is only a fraction of the representation of a person. Skills and experience are less important than values and personality.

As I stated in Chapter 2, "You can teach skills but you can't teach personality." You can grow a person's skills to the level you need them to be, but you typically can't improve or change a person's personality. "You can't teach employees to smile. They have to smile before you hire them," according to business leader Arte Nathan.

This principle is exemplified in the book, *The Ideal Team Player*, by business management expert Patrick Lencioni. The book suggests that three specific qualities are required in order to have an ideal team member: being humble, hungry and smart. A person who has humility often praises others, gives credit to the team members, and isn't out for herself. A team member who is hungry has a strong work ethic and seeks to accomplish what needs to be accomplished. A team member who is smart has deep emotional intelligence, is perceptive of others, and truly listens to what others are saying.

If we have a candidate who has outstanding skills but doesn't fit our values we simply won't hire him. If we find another candidate who lacks a bit of experience but perfectly fits our values, we'll choose this second candidate every time. Author and speaker Simon Sinek says it well, "You don't hire for skills, you hire for attitude. You can always teach skills."

It's also important to hire people that you and your team members like. The professionals that you let into your organization will spend innumerable hours interacting with you and your team. You wouldn't purposely spend a great deal of time with someone who's negative or unlikable in your personal life. Why should you allow someone who your team doesn't like into your organization? Sometimes a candidate checks all the right boxes but there's something not quite right. You have a lingering doubt and you're seeing red flags. In my experience, your gut feeling is usually right.

As they say, "One bad apple spoils the bunch." When you screen potential candidates, you must focus on the cultural impact they will have on your organization. You must ensure every person who joins will add to your positive culture, not take away. You must thoroughly screen each person who may join your team. Adding likable, friendly, positive people to your team is a recipe for strong company culture.

Business and leadership expert Brian Tracy summarized the art of hiring well when he said, "Hire as much for attitude, personality, and character as you do for job skills. Make sure that the new person will fit in comfortably with your company culture and work well with yourself and others. If you select people with the right attitude and personality, you can train and manage them to do the job well."

Potent Questions to Ask Job Candidates

A recent survey showed that 78 percent of job candidates admit they did or would consider misrepresenting themselves on their application.[14] Put another way, just one in six job seekers say they didn't stretch the truth during their hiring experience.

Finding the right team members is hard. How can you select the best employees if they aren't always honest?

One of the keys is to accept that hiring isn't a cure for your current troubles. Adding an employee isn't a quick fix for the current problem but a long-term solution for growth. Hiring shouldn't be rushed. Employers that take the time to do their research, spend vast amounts of time with the candidate, ask difficult questions, and make expectations clear are the winners.

With this in mind, you must discover the values of your candidate and examine how he will mesh with your organization's values. You can discover this by asking him directly or by listening for themes in the interviews. I recently interviewed someone who continually referred to his wife and kids. Clearly, the love of family is an important value to him. In another interview, I heard a young woman repeatedly bring up how she felt she didn't have a voice at her current job and how she wanted to contribute and be heard. Obviously, communication and listening are things she deeply values.

Ensure your company values are clearly understood by the candidate. Ask questions based on these values. Ask which of the values resonate most and why. Seek examples of how she has displayed a certain value in the past. Your values are your first defense against the encroachment of a negative workplace. Use them as guideposts to evaluate who is the right and wrong fit for your team.

As Tony Hsieh said, "It's really important to come up with core values that you can commit to. And by commit, we mean that you're willing to hire and fire based on them. If you're willing to do that, then you're well on your way to building a company culture that is in line with the brand you want to build."

When interviewing, ask behavioral questions instead of hypothetical questions. "Tell me about a time…" is better than, "What would you do if…" As business management expert Peter Drucker said, "Only past performance is an accurate predictor of future performance."

Here are a few good interview questions that can provide insights into the values and the personality of your job candidate:

- What are you most passionate about in the workplace?
- In what ways would your friends say that you could improve?
- What's your workplace pet peeve?
- What are three things we should know about working with you?
- Tell me about someone who is better than you in an area that really matters to you.
- What are you best at?
- Which of our company values is most important to you?
- Which of our company values is least important to you?
- What are three words your friends would use to describe you?

Finally, don't underestimate the power of references. What other people say about someone is often more accurate and insightful than what she says about herself. Reach out to her references and ask about her values. What do friends or past coworkers say about the type of person she is and what's most important to her? Will she exemplify your values? Which of your values will she struggle with the most?

Should You Really Hire Slow, Fire Fast?

A boss I once had would occasionally brag that his company had never fired an employee. That certainly sounds impressive, but is it? I remember one employee in particular that could never seem to complete his work, arrived late every day, and loved passing along gossip. For years he caused numerous issues that frustrated many of us. He was talked to but was never let go. You may have a similar person at your organization.

When an employee is creating issues, the organization should do everything possible to work with that person, help him improve, keep expectations clear, and communicate what needs to be done for employment to continue. Many employees can overcome their weaknesses and grow into capable workers. Some employees, however, cannot or will not improve. Sometimes it's essential to release someone.

We recently interviewed and hired a new team member who seemed like a great fit. He said all the right things, his personality was fantastic, his skills seemed ideal, his references checked out, and he seemed excited about working with us.

After the first month, however, it became apparent we had a few issues. His skills were clearly not where we thought they were. We worked diligently with him for the next two months, offering guidance and training and having weekly meetings with him. While he was good at receiving feedback, he wouldn't change his behavior. After 90 days, it became clear that this wasn't going to work and we had to release him.

Our employee retention rate is high and we rarely have to fire someone. But even we are not perfect. In fact, no company is perfect at hiring. It's impossible to hire the exact perfect person every time. It doesn't matter how good you or your team is, there will eventually be someone who joins your team that doesn't fit.

I once spoke with a young leader who was having tremendous difficulties reigning in an employee. For years, his company's culture had suffered because of the situation. He had worked with the employee, provided training, and had tough conversations, but nothing worked. He didn't know what to do.

"If you let this employee go, it would be extremely difficult," I said, "but what would your company be like a year after this employee was gone?" His eyes lit up. "It would be incredible!"

It's easy to allow a bad employee to stay. It's difficult to release him. If you have someone who is decreasing morale, creating problems, and harming the overall culture, you must take action. Either he leaves or other employees will start to leave because of him. If you're in a corporation, HR and Legal will push back, trying to avoid a firing, but press on. Have the hard conversation. Make expectations clear. Provide a bullet point list of improvements that must occur by a certain date. Check in with him regularly. Finally, if improvement doesn't occur, release him to other opportunities. Your team will thank you and someday, he may as well.

In his book, *Good to Great,* Jim Collins states it simply: "Get the right people on the bus, get the right people into the right seats on the bus, and then get the wrong people off the bus."

MAJOR TAKEAWAYS

- Nothing impacts your company culture more than the people who comprise it.
- The individuals who join your department or company must be a cultural fit.

- A job candidate's personality must be the right fit. You can usually grow a person's skills to the level you need them to be, but you typically can't improve or change a person's personality.
- The most important thing to do during the job interview process is to ensure the candidate's values sync with your organization's values.
- Listen to your gut when interviewing. If a candidate checks all the right boxes but something doesn't feel quite right, look into it.
- Hire people that you and your team members like.
- One bad apple spoils the bunch. If an employee isn't working out and won't improve, release that person.

CHAPTER 8
HOW TO BUILD AN INCREDIBLE REMOTE WORKPLACE CULTURE

"Good communication is the bridge between confusion and clarity." - Nat Turner

Did you attend college in person? If you did, you probably have plenty of memories: all night cramming for an exam, that one professor with all the weird theories, tailgating at football games, playing pranks on your roommate, etc. Now consider the experience of someone who attends an online university. While the education received may be similar, which experience do you think is more impactful? Which is more memorable? Are alumni who attended remotely or in person more likely to donate to their college?

All my college classes were in-person except one. I had one online art class. I never met the professor, nor did I ever interact with the students. Other than several emails and messages, it was an isolating experience. Of course, this was a number of years ago, and the technology wasn't what it is today, but I never built relationships in the class. Today, I have almost no memories of the experience.

While all the principles shared in this book are meant to be applicable to in-person, remote and hybrid teams, working from home does bring about unique circumstances.

Building a great company culture is almost always more difficult when your team is in remote or hybrid. The personal connection simply isn't the same. Spontaneous conversations don't erupt the same way they do when in person. Brainstorming isn't as dynamic. People are less likely to be engaged when in an online group meeting. Non-verbal cues, expressions and body language aren't perceived the same when you're being rendered as pixels on a screen.

Additionally, remote work environments are very similar. It's more difficult for your organization's culture to stand out when the experience for the employee is at the same kitchen table he would sit at for any other remote job. There's less to differentiate you from the competition.

Another complication that can arise from remote working is mental health struggles. While any working environment can provide challenges, many studies are showing the isolation and lack of community experienced when working at home can have a heavy impact.

A recent survey by the American Psychiatric Association showed the majority of employees working from home say they experienced negative mental health impacts, including isolation, loneliness, and difficulty getting away from work at the end of the day.[15] Another survey showed that seven in 10 remote employees are feeling more isolated compared to being in the office. Additionally, two-thirds said they work directly with someone they wouldn't be able to pick out of a lineup and recognize by name only.[16]

Many who work at home have also struggled with stepping away from their work. More than two-thirds of employees who work from home at least part of the time report they have trouble getting away from work at the end of the day.[17]

Remote workers also face the risk of being the first to go if layoffs occur. When tasked with the removal of employees, it's typically easier for managers to select people with whom they have less of a connection. In a recent survey, 60 percent of managers said that remote workers would probably be laid off first.[18] It's simply easier to cut ties with a person digitally than in person.

Does all this mean it's impossible to have a positive, supportive remote workplace? Absolutely not. It is possible, but it takes additional communication, support, and strategy.

Give Remote Workers Strong Communication and Relationship Building

As emphasized in chapter five, clear and constant communication is one of the bedrocks of a strong workplace. This is especially true if your team is remote.

When working from home, your employees don't get the same relationship-building benefit of spontaneous conversations. While this type of small talk can still occur, the feeling of connection is often missed because meetings and calls are focused on topics and allow less personal connection. When remote, people don't run into each other in the kitchen, share a laugh in the hallway, or gather to watch a funny video together. While this may seem like a positive that allows for more time for productivity to some bosses, it reduces the time for relationships to flourish amongst team members.

Remember, if you want an incredible work environment, you've got to take the time to not focus on "business." Take time to connect with people. Regardless of your role, getting to know your coworkers is always worth it. We all work harder when we feel we're supporting people we care about. Employees will be less likely to leave if they have solid friendships at work.

My wife has worked remotely for many years, leading teams of professionals miles away from each other. She's passionate about this principle, and spends hours of time each week on individual one-on-one calls with her team members. She is constantly touching base, listening, asking questions, and building relationships. She'll randomly send a gift card or flowers to a team member paid for with her own money. She plans regular virtual games and happy hours meant just for fun and connection.

If your team is remote, your managers simply can't afford to be "all business." They must personally take the time to connect more with team members and encourage others to do the same. This requires more time than it does with in-person teams because the natural flow of information simply isn't the same as it is when people are physically together.

Can your organization save money by going remote not having an office? Of course. But it should use these financial savings to give managers more daily time to manage.

Remote Teams Can't Afford to Skip the Joy
Even if you're not at the same physical location, experiencing jovial joy is essential for your team. Be purposeful about planning

regular events that are not focused on clients, work, deadlines, or billable hours. This may be weekly, bi-weekly or whatever works for your organization.

When you schedule a virtual meeting that has a clear purpose of fun, you give participants permission to let their hair down. Set the tone by being jovial. Joke, laugh, and tease your team members (in a friendly, nice way, of course). But what should you plan for the agenda of the meeting?

One idea is a virtual lunch or happy hour. Schedule a half hour or an hour and ask everyone to bring a lunch or drink of their choice. If you have a small team or department, everyone can join. If your team is larger, assign smaller groups beforehand. Selecting the right people for each group is important. Ensure you have at least one or two people in each group who are talkative and will keep the conversation going. Don't include people together just because they're friends. This is an opportunity to get people who don't normally connect to get to know each other.

A piece of advice: politely encourage everyone to turn on their cameras. While many people prefer to keep their camera off and communicate on video calls via audio only, everyone will be able to better connect when they're able to see each other. If you're a leader (or want to be one), you should always have your video on and allow your team and clients to see you.

The agenda for the lunch or happy hour is simple: enjoy a little food or drink and talk. For some teams, this is the recipe for the perfect team-building experience filled with great conversation and laughs. Every team is different, however, and some groups may struggle to find good conversation along the way. If you fear this may be the case, provide a list of ten questions to one person in each group and ask him to run through the questions with the group. This is a simple but wonderful way to keep the conversation going, generate laughs, and allow everyone to learn more about each other.

Here are a few example questions I've used to generate great conversation:

- What's the strangest job you've ever had?
- Who has had the most broken bones?
- What would be a great tagline for _____? (choose one participant in the group)
- What was the last dream you had about work?
- If one person in the office had to give everyone haircuts, who would you choose?
- What's the grossest thing you used to enjoy eating in elementary school?

Note these questions aren't typical conversation starters. Simple questions like, "What's your favorite sports team?" are fine, but they don't have as much potential to generate unusual or humorous conversation as, "What's the grossest thing you used to enjoy eating in elementary school?" Answers to a question like this are more interesting and memorable (I asked this question once, and someone on our team answered that she used to "lick the inside of popcorn bags," while another would "drink buttermilk by the glass").

Another good way to add a little joy to your remote team is a virtual game. There are innumerable options for a game, but trivia is one of the easiest to set up and administer. You can find trivia questions about topics like movies, pop culture, or even your industry, but I've found greater results when I create custom questions about our team members. The personalization makes the game more interesting, and your team members will appreciate the extra effort. I've worked with most of our team members for many years, so I remember many quirky and interesting facts about them that make for wonderful questions. If that's not the case for you, send out a message a few days ahead of time and ask each team member to share a few weird facts about themselves, then compile them into questions.

Other great game options include online versions of Pictionary, bingo, Battleship, charades, or telephone. Crowdpurr is a great online trivia game for remote teams. My wife often uses Jackbox games like Quiplash or Drawful with her team. A search for "online games for remote teams" will give you other good options.

No matter what type of game you choose, make things a little more interesting by including some sort of prize for the winner. A gift card, extra PTO, some company swag or any sort of gift for the winner will up the stakes and make the experience a little better.

But what if team members don't want to join another meeting, even if it is meant to be fun? While I don't think it's beneficial to ever force someone to participate in a fun event, you should encourage everyone to join. If someone isn't interested in doing so, talk to him one-on-one and explain why this is important.

When team members spend time together while not focusing on work, they will grow closer, bond with one another, and appreciate each other more. The commitment to have fun together is simply one of the smartest business decisions a team can make.

Even Remote Teams Must Meet Face-to-Face

Each August, my wife, Melíssa, invites her team to the Iowa State Fair. If you're unfamiliar with this legendary midwestern tradition, the Iowa State Fair is Iowa's largest celebration, annually attracting over a million people from all over the world. It showcases the state's best in agriculture, industry, and entertainment. National media frequently rank the fair as one of the top events in the country. It features all the rides, livestock, shows, and attractions you might expect, but perhaps the greatest draw of the fair is its unique food offerings. Last year it featured tasty delicacies such as rattlesnake corndogs, butter on a stick and Icelandic fermented shark on a stick.

Melíssa's team is primarily in New York and Boston, so joining us in Iowa is a unique experience for them. The first year they visited, only one or two of the ten team members had ever been to the Midwest. Melíssa was very purposeful with the time she had with her team. They had two days of working together in person and a few days focused on fun and team building. She planned activities like an epic team scavenger hunt through the fairgrounds, a massive water fight at her parent's farm with 15,000 water balloons, an afternoon enjoying all-you-can-eat free sweetcorn at the Adel Sweetcorn Festival, and evenings out with dinner and karaoke.

The impact this experience made was significant. Everyone on the trip bonded and created unique memories with each other. They went back to their regular remote working schedule, motivated and strengthened by the experience. Everyone knew each other a little better and cared a bit more. It was an incredible team-building trip.

While you don't need to plan a trip this bold, you will get great results from bringing remote team members together. Whether you do it monthly, quarterly, or annually, meeting in person is worth it. Yes, it takes time and money, but this isn't just an expense, it's an investment.

Consider when and how your department or team can get together in person. While some of the time can be centered on productivity or learning, ensure most of it is focused on fun. Your goal is for everyone to leave with positive memories and a greater understanding of each other.

If, for some reason, bringing your team or department together in person isn't an option, consider visiting them yourself. Have a couple of employees in Ohio? Plan a trip to spend the day with them. Work with someone who's three hours away? Drive out and have lunch with him.

People naturally feel closer and more engaged with someone sitting in the same room, rather than a person who exists merely on a screen. Nothing can substitute for a face-to-face meeting to build trust and a relationship.

The Danger of a Hybrid Workplace Culture

With the rise of today's hybrid workplaces, a new danger has emerged: a single company with two cultures. It can be easy to begin treating in-person employees and fully remote employees differently. Communicating with one group may be easier than the other, which can slowly cause a divide.

As discussed in Chapter 5, when a few people intentionally or unintentionally form a group that views others as opposition, trouble is on the horizon. Both in-person and remote employees will have different experiences; this is unavoidable and one of the risks of a hybrid workplace. But your leadership must be purposeful about uniting employees in and out of the office.

Your managers should recognize the fact that remote workers often feel more disconnected and will likely require more communication and support. When people feel connected to their leaders, they have more trust in their organizations.

Closely monitor your hybrid culture. Encourage leaders to be impartial, treat both groups as equally as possible, and continue to communicate frequently and positively. Find opportunities for those in the office to work and bond with those working from home. Bring people together in real life when possible. Hybrid offices that regularly connect teams together in person have a greater chance of keeping a single, unified culture.

MAJOR TAKEAWAYS

- Building a great company culture is almost always more difficult when your team is remote.
- Clear and constant communication is absolutely essential when managing a remote team.
- Remote teams should schedule regular virtual events focused on getting to know one another and having fun.
- Whether you do it monthly, quarterly or annually, remote teams will gain great benefits from meeting regularly in person.
- Nothing can substitute for a face-to-face meeting to build trust and a relationship.
- Closely monitor hybrid workplaces to ensure two separate cultures are not being formed.

CHAPTER 9

HOW A STRONG COMPANY CULTURE WILL ATTRACT TALENT AND BUSINESS

"Hiring people is an art, not a science, and resumes can't tell you whether someone will fit into a company's culture." – Howard Schultz

In chapter four, I shared the story of how we secretly met our team members' parents in order to learn more about them and create a surprise for the team. While this was a very genuine gesture done purely for our team members, everyone loved the experience so much that we eventually decided to make it public.

We took the original 30-minute video and cut it down to a brief version, then placed the shortened, employee-approved video of the experience online. The video fascinated our clients and the public. I placed it in a post on my LinkedIn account, and it began receiving thousands of views almost immediately. We received hundreds of positive comments, and a few people even told me the video made them tear up. One of our clients' Vice Presidents recently told me that they had just selected Blue Compass as their vendor when he happened across this video on LinkedIn. "After I watched that video, I knew we had selected the right vendor," he told me, "I can tell this is a company that cares about its people." I was eventually contacted by the media and interviewed about the experience.

The good news is that you don't have to plan and film an elaborate production like the "meet the parents" video to get the public's attention. Recently I posted a very brief clip of our team laughing on social media. I didn't put much thought into the post, but it garnered a great deal of attention. I was surprised by how many people commented on the post, both in the comments section of the post itself and in person. I even had a leadership podcast reach out to me for an interview because of it.

The purpose of a positive company culture is to bless your team by allowing them to enjoy their work, grow, and do their best. But another benefit of a positive work environment is the magnet it can be for new talent and business. A strong company culture is a light that can't be hidden. Employees' spouses talk about it. Clients mention it to their colleagues. It seeps out via social media.

As I mentioned, we regularly have clients compliment us on how happy and positive our team members are. People who enter our office often mention that they can feel the positive energy. We've had multiple clients tell us a major factor in the selection of our agency was because of our great culture. We win local and national awards for our incredible culture.

Everyone wants to work at a place where they can experience appreciation, growth, and great relationships. If your business is a good place to work, it's not wrong to share that with the world. As CEO of my company, I know that part of my job is to be a cheerleader for our team and our business. If you're a leader, consider ways that you can champion the excellence of your workplace. Be passionate about your brand!

But the key is to do so genuinely.

All your efforts to improve and maintain a positive company culture should be first focused on your team, not the public. You can't fake good culture. If you're putting more effort into claiming your culture is great on your website and social media than actually appreciating your team, you're doing it wrong. Be genuine in all your efforts.

Using Your Culture to Attract New Talent and Business

If you have a solid company culture, let it shine for the world to see. When you share your culture externally, potential hires and prospects get the opportunity to see what they're missing.

There are numerous ways to market your company culture. The best and most natural way is word of mouth. When your workplace is positive, your team members and clients will naturally spread the word. This is why doing the work to keep your culture strong is a fantastic, indirect marketing tactic. But your leaders should do the same. Be passionate about your culture inside and outside of your office, and others will take note.

Sharing your culture digitally is just as important as doing so in person. At Blue Compass, we always try to film interesting events, then share them on social media and YouTube. These days, the vast majority of organizations have at least one social media account. If your organization doesn't, consider starting an account to showcase your workplace adventures.

We provide digital marketing solutions to numerous organizations, and one of the most important solutions we provide is content marketing. Business owners and marketing teams often struggle to come up with content ideas for their social media accounts, blog, and YouTube channel. If you're ever concerned about being able to generate good ideas for digital content or social media posts, just remember your team members and your company culture. Don't put pressure on yourself to generate genius, viral social posts; just focus on your people and let them be the source of your content.

The best social media posts are genuine content about real people. Feature real photos of your team members. Never use stock photos. We've run dozens of A/B tests on social platforms and websites and discovered that images with real people always get more engagement than stock photos. People can tell the difference. Use authentic photos.

Your social media presence should showcase your team members. Here are a few ideas:

- Highlight people on their work anniversaries with a nice photo and a quote about how awesome that person is.
- Post a photo of some of your team having lunch together.
- Share a brief video montage of team members volunteering together at a company service day.
- Post a photo of a department getting together for a training session. Explain the value of learning and how your organization puts a priority on it.
- Shoot a three-minute video of a couple of team members (who know each other well and have good personalities) discussing an industry-relevant topic and giving away advice. This is a great way to demonstrate your company's

expertise and show off the positive interactions your employees have with one another.

- Collect quotes about what team members like most about your culture. Make graphics out of each quote and post one a week.
- Capture and share genuine reactions. For instance, a video of team members laughing together, celebrating a big win or accepting an award.

(Super social media secret: we've posted thousands of posts for clients over the years and discovered that posting photos of babies or pets always gets more clicks, likes, shares, and comments. Since we have dogs in our office every day, this works really well for us.)

Consider how you and your team members can be more alert to opportunities to take photos or videos of positive, fun moments around the office, at team events, lunches, etc. Encourage your team to send good content to the person in charge of your company's social media.

At Blue Compass, we have a special culture email address set up so that any team member can submit internal photos or videos at any time. Our social media team selects good submissions and shares them on our social platforms.

Integrating elements of your culture throughout your website is just as important. Add a company culture page that shares your organization's real approach to your work environment and highlights what makes your workplace different. Be clear about what your culture is and isn't. Include your values, add photos, embed videos, anything to give outsiders a clear picture of what it's like to be a team member. It's good to focus on the positives of your culture, but you must be truthful. It's important your website is honest about your company's culture. Just as you wouldn't lie about your products or services, you can't share falsehoods about what it's like to work at your company. Employees will resent it and new hires will quickly recognize the inconsistency.

But adding one company culture page isn't enough. Consider filling your entire website with touches of your culture. Add information about your team members on your "About Us" page. Include blog articles about unique aspects of your company or fun team events. Talk about how your employees serve your clients on your service line pages. Add real photos of your team members working together throughout the website. Your entire online presence should celebrate your people.

Another effective way to attract great talent or business prospects is to invite them to a fun team outing, lunch, or remote meeting. What better way to give someone a true taste of what it's like to be on your team than to have them experience it firsthand?

When in Doubt, be Yourself First

When sharing your culture with the world, try to capture the genuine spirit of your office and encourage team members to be themselves. A simple, universal rule of thumb is that people do business with people they like. What better way to endear yourself to clients than to be yourself, smile, and care about them?

Sometimes professionals get too professional around clients or potential hires. While a healthy dose of respect is important, encourage your team to be their authentic selves around new prospective clients or hires. If your team teases each other, perhaps some friendly teasing of clients is in order. Sure, some people are all business and have no interest in small talk or jokes, but most people enjoy a little lightheartedness in their meetings. The prospect should get a real dose of what your people are like. Don't change who you are just because a client joined the meeting or entered the office.

When a new prospective client or a job seeker comes to our office, they immediately get a heavy dose of the Blue Compass culture when two or three dogs greet them. This friendly greeting crew immediately puts most people at ease and starts the interaction off in a positive way. Is this greeting crew for everyone? Of course not; a small percentage of people don't care for these interactions with dogs. If that's the case, we simply may not be a good fit for them. We don't hide who we are.

I encourage my team members to be themselves, but be the best version of themselves. Your office will be happier when each person is authentic. As author Alan Cohen says, "Everything will line up perfectly when knowing and living the truth becomes more important than looking good."

MAJOR TAKEAWAYS

- A positive work environment doesn't just benefit the team. It's a magnet for new talent and new business.
- Share your culture with the world, but in-person and digitally.
- Your website and social media should celebrate your team members.
- Always be genuine. Encourage your team members to be themselves around new business prospects, clients, and potential hires.
- Your office will be happier when each person is authentic.

CHAPTER 10
FREQUENTLY ASKED QUESTIONS ABOUT COMPANY CULTURE

"Why is culture so important to a business? Here is a simple way to frame it. The stronger the culture, the less corporate process a company needs. When the culture is strong, you can trust everyone to do the right thing." - Brian Chesky

No matter how great your company's culture is, issues will arise. No workplace is perfect, we're all human, and every business has unique challenges.

The following are several common questions about company culture, all of which I've received at speaking events, panels, or one-on-one with business leaders.

How Can I Impact the Company Culture When I Don't Have the Power?

The principles in this book may sound great to you, but what if you're not the CEO? ...or the President? ...or a VP? ...or a manager? ...or a senior team member?

Sometimes I'm asked questions like, "but how can I change my company's culture?
I'm not a leader." It's a great question. Many of us report to managers, VPs or c-suite executives who have little interest in adding joy to the workplace. While the importance of company culture has become more evident in recent years, many leaders still put little value in such efforts.

You may not have the authority to snap your fingers and change workplace conditions, but you can make a deep impact within your sphere of influence. And your sphere can impact other spheres.

Simon Sinek stated this well in an interview, saying, "I always recommend to be the leader you wish you had… you can't control what you can't control, so worry about the people around you. Worry about the people to the sides of you, the level below you, even the level above you, and you be the leader you wish you had. What you start to find in those pockets is these magical little diamonds in the rough appear."[19]

John Maxwell's book, *The 360 Degree Leader*, is about this very topic. In it, he explains that listening to and supporting your team members will eventually bring you to the point where they are asking you for advice. This is a powerful and influential place to be. When others trust you, your ability to influence the culture for good greatly increases, regardless of your title. Relationship building is the foundation of effective leadership.

Do you have a difficult boss that puts his own ambitions above supporting the team? If so, how can you help him and make him better? Sound difficult? It probably will be. It takes a person of great character to help a difficult boss instead of gossiping about him.

How are Small Business and Corporate Culture Different?

While I believe the principles shared in this book are generally applicable no matter the size of your organization, there are certainly different elements at play when comparing the culture of a large corporation to a small business.

Most research shows company culture is better in smaller organizations. A recent study reveals that most of the employees at smaller companies (zero to 100 employees) say they have an "Awesome" company culture. On the other hand, employees at large enterprises (1,001+ employees) primarily rate their company culture as "Average."[20]

Small businesses have an advantage over large corporations in that there are fewer team members. There are not as many opinions, factions, or groups, making it easier to rally teams together and keep departments on the same page. Often, smaller organizations have better cultures because coworkers have better relationships with one another. It's tough to enjoy your job when departments are clashing and people are stealing your credit. Sadly, this is too often the case at large corporations. Culture can get even more complicated at large public corporations, where the additional pressure of pleasing stockholders with good quarterly numbers may impede leaders' focus on long-term cultural growth.

Small businesses also offer higher flexibility. If something isn't working, it can be more easily changed. There's typically not much bureaucracy. There's naturally more transparency within teams.

Communication is simpler. It's easier for team members to feel as if they have a voice.

So should you give up the good fight for great culture if you're at a large enterprise? Absolutely not. While you may have a few extra challenges, a great workplace is possible. I've seen some amazing cultures at giant companies and terrible working environments at small organizations.

Most large businesses have the advantage of being able to offer higher salaries and greater benefits. That's definitely a positive in attracting and retaining talent, but, as we discussed in chapter one, great company culture is not tangible benefits. It is easier for a large company to offer experiences like memorable team outings or fulfilling volunteering experiences. They may be able to offer support to employees that smaller businesses can't afford, such as job training, conferences, leadership coaches and therapists. While these benefits don't guarantee a better workplace, they can add to a more fulfilling culture.

The key to great culture in corporate environments is employing and empowering great managers and focusing on the individual cultures of departments or teams. Don't worry as much about the company culture as a whole; that will take care of itself if individual groups are unified and supported. Ensure the managers of each department not only emphasize positive relationships within each group but are committed to unity with other departments as well.

How Can Our Small Business Compete for Talent When Big Corporations Offer Huge Benefits?

It's not all sunshine and rainbows for small businesses. I've owned a small business for many years and I know the struggles, one of which can be the competition against corporations for the best talent. Sure, smaller businesses may have the advantage when it comes to culture, but large companies often look very attractive to those seeking new opportunities.

"How do we compete with the large companies that offer huge salaries and have full gyms for employees?" a woman once asked me during a Q & A after a speech.

"Now that big corporations like Google are hiring regionally, how do we compete?" I was recently asked while on a company culture panel.

Most large companies have a major advantage over smaller companies: more resources. Again, corporations can typically offer higher salaries, longer maternity leave, better health care, a higher 401k match, etc.

While that might seem like an insurmountable edge if you're trying to build a team at a small organization, you have an advantage that many large companies lack: more flexibility, less bureaucracy, greater transparency, and more frequent communication. The truth is that a supportive, positive, communicative culture that truly values each individual team member is an experience that few corporations can compete with. I believe it's worth more than that extra salary or company gym.

But how can you make top talent aware of your positive company culture? How can you use your great workplace as a tool to attract great prospects? The answer is in Chapter 9: let your culture shine. Share it with the world. Allow job prospects to visit your office, talk with your team members, and join a company event. Share your positive job retention stats. Be a cheerleader for your culture.

How Long Does it Take to Reverse a Toxic Company Culture?

This is a natural question. If your goal is to fix a negative workplace, you've accepted an admirable task, but how long is this going to take?

There's no easy answer, unfortunately, as there are so many elements at play when considering an organization's culture. The ease and duration of your task depend on many factors, including:

- The size of your organization
- The structure of your organization
- The quality of your leader
- The general workload put on employees
- The values of your organization and the importance placed on those values
- The quality of the character of your employees
- The quality and influence of your clients
- The policies of your organization
- The history and internal perception of your organization

The bottom line is that it takes time to reverse a toxic culture. It may take six months. It may take six years. Don't let the time investment intimidate you. That time will pass regardless of your efforts. You might as well work on the culture. Focus on what you can change. Spend time on what will make the greatest impact.

Improving your culture can improve your profitability, boost everyone's quality of life and of course, retain great talent. It's worth it and you can do it.

Our Office is Overworked and Undersupported - Can We Have a Good Culture Under These Conditions?

Many marketing agencies are known for making their team members work 50 or 60 hours per week. We have a competitor who regularly pushes employees to hit 70 hours. Indeed, this is a profitable strategy for a business …in the short term.

All companies will hit times when extra work from employees is necessary. I believe that's reasonable and acceptable, but only if it's for a season. Working a 50-hour week a few times a year is one thing, but there's a problem if your team members are doing it every week. Your organization will never have a truly great culture until everyone has a reasonable workload.

"Burnout is nature's way of telling you you've been going through the motions your soul has departed," according to author Sam Keen. When real burnout begins to impact your team members, your culture is in a dangerous place.

If this is an issue at your organization, tackle it immediately. I don't know what the perfect solution is for your business, but I believe the issue won't solve itself without a strong strategy and action. Hiring more people is expensive. Taking less work is risky. Stepping in and helping do the work yourself is time-intensive. Reevaluating your processes is difficult. Yet these may be solutions worth implementing before your team starts looking elsewhere.

We're Busy and Can't Afford to Lose Anyone, but We Have Someone Who is a Bad Apple and is Ruining Our Culture

I recently sat down with a leader who shared this sentiment with me. One of her employees was complaining, gossiping, and negatively impacting her company's culture, but he was getting work done, and they simply couldn't afford to lose anyone due to their workload.

"Either he leaves, or your other employees start leaving," I said.

If you have a team member who won't improve and clearly needs to go, every day you delay taking action is a risk. One of the biggest travesties in business is when a bad team member causes a good team member to leave.

As I mentioned in the introduction, as a young leader I hired a number of people who were a poor fit for our culture. Thus, we had to eventually let quite a few toxic people go over the years. This was difficult, but I've never regretted it once. In fact, after the person left and the dust settled, I always found myself wishing I had taken action sooner. Somehow, the work continued to get done, and we were able to hire someone who was a much better fit for the role.

Be bold, take action, defend your culture, and retain valuable team members. Remove the bad apple. You won't regret it.

This Company Culture Stuff Sounds too Cheesy and Fluffy

"No one cares about axe throwing," the VP indignantly announced to me, "why do we have to have all these company events?!" I had been asked to consult with her organization on company culture. While she liked a lot of what we had to say, it was clear she loathed the efforts her team made to get together outside of work. The recent axe-throwing event had brought many of her team members together, but she resented the pressure she received to go to these events. "It's fluffy nonsense," she pouted.

Some people feel all this company culture stuff is fluffy, shallow gestures that have no real impact. The story about how I wrote humorous poems for each of our team members in Chapter 3, for instance. What a waste of time, right? Do such silly, cheesy efforts really make an impact?

It's true that these "fluffy" gestures aren't for everyone. In fact, some of your employees may roll their eyes when they receive a heartfelt note on their desk. But they do resonate with many of your team members.

Just because you don't care for a certain language of appreciation doesn't mean everyone feels the same way. As I mentioned in Chapter 3, not everyone values the same type of acknowledgement. Each person in your organization is different, and some forms of appreciation may be much more valued by an individual than others. If you express appreciation in ways that aren't meaningful to your team members, they may not feel valued. This is because you and your coworkers are likely speaking different languages.

Don't look down on gestures of appreciation that aren't your cup of tea. If your company plans a happy hour, consider attending, even if it's not your favorite activity. If your team goes paintballing and you have little interest, think about showing up for at least one round. If you receive a cheesy poem and aren't impressed, feel thankful anyway.

If you're a leader, or seek to be, it's especially important for you to be supportive of different extracurricular activities and appreciation in the office, and you must encourage your managers to support all the company's attempts to acknowledge team members. Embrace a culture-building attempt that you don't find particularly interesting because for some people that attempt is deeply meaningful.

What's the Number One Thing We Can do to Make the Greatest Positive Impact on Company Culture?

Recently, a few leaders at a large corporation asked me to meet at a coffee shop and answer a few of their questions about company culture. They had described their culture as "toxic," so I was interested to hear more about the situation. About 20 minutes into our conversation, an older woman suddenly approached and sat down in the empty seat at our table. She was the company's President.

While I appreciated the opportunity to meet with the President, it was soon clear that she wasn't particularly interested in my advice and had shown up just to appease her fellow leaders. She was convinced that the solution to their toxic workplace was simple: let go of five bad employees. "Fire those idiots!" she angrily grumbled. Her team members agreed that might be necessary, but first they wanted a solid plan and strategy to improve their culture moving forward. "I don't know why this is so hard for you," she said. "Fire them!" She wasn't interested in any other strategies.

Clearly, there are innumerable elements that impact the quality of your workplace, but the five keys I've shared are the foundation of a solid company culture. If your organization can implement Visible Values, Appreciative Acknowledgement, Jovial Joy, Constant Connections, and Genuine Growth, it will be a quality workplace that attracts and retains great talent.

But what if you could only change one thing about your company culture? What's the one element that has the greatest impact on the work environment of an organization?

The number one thing you can do to improve company culture is to ensure you have a positive, supportive leader. The impact that the leader has on an organization is tremendous. I shared this quote earlier, but it bears repeating: "Every CEO is, in fact, a Chief Cultural Officer. The terrifying thing is it's the CEO's actual behavior, not their speeches or the list of values they have put up on posters, that defines what the culture is."

The companies that are winning the culture game benefit from servant leaders who put their team before themselves. As John Maxwell says, "A good leader is a person who takes a little more than his share of the blame and a little less than his share of the credit."

It's the leader that has the greatest impact in pushing the Five Keys of Incredible Company Culture forward. Additionally, note that these keys aren't just qualities of a good culture but character traits of a great leader. The culture of a company is a reflection of its leaders.

If you're a leader, it may be time to step up your game. If your boss is the leader, encourage her, help her, and share these keys with her. If your boss is a lost cause who cares only for profits and not people, it may be time to look for other opportunities.

How Can I be Free of the Fear of Employees Leaving?
Ah, the magical, wonderful word that's music to leaders' ears: "RETAIN."

We all want our team members to stay. We want them to enjoy their experience and produce great work. We don't want to face the time and cost and struggle to replace them.

It's natural for leaders to fear the loss of great people. So how can you avoid this fear? By doing two things:

First, genuinely work to move your culture in the right direction. Share the concepts in this book with your leadership team and your managers, and get to work.

Second, accept that people will leave.

I know; the book is titled "*RETAIN.*" Should I really be saying that? The truth is, you'll never be able to keep everyone from leaving.

Life happens. Even if you have a 100 percent perfect company culture, someone will have to leave for health reasons. Someone will leave when her husband gets a new job in another state. Someone will leave when he retires. Someone will leave when she chooses to stay home and be a full-time mom.

The right question for organizations to be asking isn't, "How do we stop employees from leaving?" We should instead be asking, "How can we allow good people to grow, flourish and enjoy their work?" It's not your job to keep people from leaving. It's your job to give them reasons to stay.

Cast aside your fears and worries. Simply do your best to create the most positive, supportive work environment you can.

And if someone does leave, express gratitude for the incredible partnership you had. Be thankful for the time he spent with you. Wish him the very best and move forward.

MAJOR TAKEAWAYS

- You may not have the authority to change workplace conditions, but you can make a deep impact within your sphere of influence. And your sphere can impact others' spheres.
- The key to great culture in corporate environments is employing and empowering great managers and focusing on the individual cultures of departments or teams.
- Burnout must be addressed immediately. When burnout begins to impact your team members, your culture is in a dangerous place.
- Feel-good, "fluffy" gestures aren't for everyone, but they can be very effective with many of your team members.
- If you're a leader, it's especially important for you to be supportive of different extracurricular activities and appreciation efforts, even if they aren't your cup of tea.
- The number one thing you can do to improve company culture is ensure you have a positive, supportive leader.
- It's not your job to keep people from leaving. It's your job to give them reasons to stay.

CONCLUSION

I've had hundreds of coffee meetings over the years. Whether with an old friend or a new contact I've never met before, I always enjoy spending time with someone in a coffee shop in the morning.

A few days before the writing of this section, I was scheduled to meet a man named Chase. We had connected on LinkedIn but had never met in person. I dropped off my boys at school and rushed to the coffee shop, arriving a few minutes late. Noticing Chase sitting at a small table by the window, I walked over, greeted him, and offered to buy him coffee. He ordered a chocolate mocha; I got an iced tea (I don't drink coffee) and we sat down.

"Tell me your story!" I prompted, "How did you get to where you are today?" He started in on his background in pharmaceutical sales, which I found interesting as it was a very different role from his current role, a program manager.

He talked about his career journey for about ten minutes, when suddenly someone approached and said, "Hi, Drew!" I turned to the side to see it was Chase. I was having coffee with the wrong guy.

I immediately realized I should have been more thorough in my selection of "Chase." Both men looked similar and had full beards. Now this guy's strange background was starting to make sense.

Just then, Jared, a friend of mine, showed up. "Hey, Drew! Do you know Joseph?" Jared was the guy who was supposed to be meeting Joseph (fake Chase), and Joseph thought I was Jared.

It was a tornado of awkwardness.

I had two choices: I could have felt embarrassed, confused, remorseful, and negative about the situation. And I would have a few years ago. But I've been around long enough to know that's not helpful. Those feelings are coming from my pride. Instead I just laughed at myself. I recovered, and we all went on with our coffee meetings (but with the correct person this time).

Nearly every issue we humans face comes from pride. "Where there is strife, there is pride, but wisdom is found in those who take advice," according to Proverbs 13:10.

Humans are imperfect. No organization, company, business, tribe, or family will ever be in perfect harmony. We are fallen, fallible creatures who require the combination of a strong value system, hope, and leadership to be our best.

People aren't just seeking a paycheck; they're seeking something they can believe in. What people value in a workplace has changed. We want more from our jobs today than we ever have before.

A positive, supportive company culture that doesn't take itself too seriously is the answer. You *can* experience a better workplace that improves morale, loyalty, and the bottom line. You can attract and retain amazing employees without worrying about them leaving.

A "Blue Compass Culture" is a joyful workplace with clear values, where team members experience incredible connections, appreciation, and growth. It isn't a perfect work environment. That doesn't exist. But it is a workplace that attracts great talent while keeping people who love drama and gossip away.

You can create an incredible company culture that no one wants to leave.

It takes a purposeful plan. It takes time. It takes solid leadership. It takes ongoing work. But it's absolutely worth it.

Because,

Working at a positive, supportive company is a truly amazing experience.

Need a hand with your company culture journey? Reach out to me at **drewharden.com**. I'd love to serve your organization.

THE INCREDIBLE CULTURE CHECKLIST

Here is the essential checklist for a great workplace. Keep these elements within your organization and you'll move towards a positive, fun, supportive work environment with supportive team members.

THE FIVE KEYS OF INCREDIBLE COMPANY CULTURE

1. **Visible Values** - A clear set of values that everyone knows and are modeled by leadership.

2. **Appreciative Acknowledgment** - An atmosphere of supportive encouragement in which all team members are quick to give credit to others.

3. **Jovial Joy** - A company-wide commitment to look on the bright side and embrace fun with leadership team members that don't take themselves too seriously.

4. **Constant Connection** - A commitment to communicate with employees, set clear expectations and regularly check-in with each team member.

5. **Genuine Growth** - A pledge to provide opportunities for all team members to improve personally and professionally.

Lastly, remember that these keys aren't just qualities of a good culture, but character traits of a great leader. Strong, servant leadership is the glue that holds a positive culture together.

ABOUT THE AUTHOR

Author, speaker, and CEO & Founder of Blue Compass, Drew Harden inspires and equips leaders to create workplaces where people experience joy and growth.

He has grown and guided Blue Compass from a two-person start-up in 2007 to one of the Midwest's leading digital marketing companies today. Drew regularly speaks at conferences around the country, has been cited by publications like USA Today, and serves clients like Spalding Sports Equipment, NAPA Auto Parts, and the NFL. He provides company culture consulting for organizations looking to make their workplace more positive and productive.

Drew lives in Des Moines, Iowa with his wife Melíssa, their two boys, Ethan and Chase, and their two huskies, Zion and Knight.

Learn more about Drew at **www.drewharden.com**

BIBLIOGRAPHY

1. DepEmployee Tenure Summary, 2020 - https://www.bls.gov/news.release/tenure.nr0.htm
2. Roughly 47 million people quit their jobs last year: 'All of this is uncharted territory' - 2022 - https://www.cnbc.com/2022/02/01/roughly-47-million-people-quit-their-job-last-year.html
3. 40% of workers are considering quitting their jobs soon—here's where they're going - 2022 - https://www.cnbc.com/2022/07/20/40percent-of-workers-are-considering-quitting-their-jobs-soon.html
4. Workers Value a Strong Company Culture Over Higher Pay, 2019 - https://www.cnbc.com/2019/07/11/workers-value-a-strong-company-culture-over-higher-pay-study-claims.html
5. *The Best Place to Work*, Chapter 7, 2014
6. O.C. Tanner Research, Performance Accelerated - https://www.octanner.com/content/dam/oc-tanner/documents/global-research/White_Paper_Performance_Accelerated.pdf
7. Employee Recognition: Low Cost, High Impact, 2016 - https://www.gallup.com/workplace/236441/employee-recognition-low-cost-high-impact.aspx
8. 10 Shocking Workplace Stats You Need To Know - https://www.forbes.com/sites/davidsturt/2018/03/08/10-shocking-workplace-stats-you-need-to-know
9. 10 Shocking Workplace Stats You Need to Know - https://www.forbes.com/sites/davidsturt/2018/03/08/10-shocking-workplace-stats-you-need-to-know/
10. Gen. Z Is Challenging the Status Quo When It Comes to Pay Transparency -

https://www.recruiter.com/recruiting/gen-z-is-challenging-the-status-quo-when-it-comes-to-pay-transparency/

11. How Vulnerability Fuels Connecting, Engagement and Results - https://corporatesolutions.johnmaxwell.com/blog/how-vulnerability-fuels-connecting-engagement-and-results/

12. Why Embracing Lifelong Learning Results in Greatness for your Start Up (or Empire) - https://medium.com/know/why-embracing-lifelong-learning-as-a-leader-results-in-greatness-for-your-organisation-or-empire-4abca9cf122d

13. 7 Steps to Nailing Staff Training and Development - https://www.perkbox.com/uk/resources/blog/7-steps-to-nailing-staff-training-and-development

14. 78% of job seekers lie during the hiring process—here's what happened to 4 of them - https://www.cnbc.com/2020/02/19/how-many-job-seekers-lie-on-their-job-application.html

15. New Research Shows Remote And Hybrid Workers Suffering Physical And Mental Health Dilemmas - https://www.forbes.com/sites/bryanrobinson/2021/11/01/new-research-shows-remote-and-hybrid-workers-suffering-physical-and-mental-health-dilemmas/

16. Two-thirds of Remote Workers Can't Recognize Anyone They Work With https://uk.news.yahoo.com/news/two-thirds-remote-workers-cant-152800925.html

17. Remote Workers Report Negative Mental Health Impacts, New Study Finds - https://www.forbes.com/sites/bryanrobinson/2021/10/15/remote-workers-report-negative-mental-health-impacts-new-study-finds/

18. Remote Workers Could be the First to Go in the Next Round of Recession Layoffs -

https://www.latimes.com/politics/story/2022-10-26/remote-workers-may-be-the-first-let-go-in-recession-related-layoffs

19. Simon Sinek Top Leadership & Psychology Skills - https://youtu.be/N8tjj9wf9VI
20. Why Smaller Companies Have Better Culture - https://www.hi5.team/blog/why-smaller-companies-have-better-culture

www.ingramcontent.com/pod-product-compliance
Lightning Source LLC
Chambersburg PA
CBHW070346220526
45467CB00001B/268